DOWN HOME
SOUTHERN COOKING

DOWN HOME SOUTHERN COOKING

by LaMont Burns

Wash Drawings by Earl Thollander

DOUBLEDAY & COMPANY, INC.
Garden City, New York

First Edition

1987

For more information about LaMont's Barbecue products or
about his franchises, write to

LaMont Burns
392 North El Camino Real
Encinitas, California 92024

Designed by Virginia M. Soulé

Library of Congress Cataloging in Publication Data

Burns, LaMont.
  Down home southern cooking.

  Includes index.
  1. Cookery, American—Southern style. 2. Cookery,
Afro-American. I. Title.
TX715.B959   1986   641.5975   86-11448
ISBN 0-385-19748-9

To my mother, Thelma . . . and in memory of my grand-mother, Ausiebelle Macklin Beaver . . . and great-grandmother, Lu-cinda Macklin.

Thank you for my culinary heritage.

CONTENTS

INTRODUCTION

When I was a little boy just starting school, I was shocked that so many of my black classmates knew absolutely nothing about their own history. I'm not talking about book learning. I'm talking about oral history, their family's histories from older relatives. The history of my own family had been drummed into me almost from the day I learned my last name.

My grandmother, Ausiebelle, and my mother, Thelma, were both cooks and I was literally raised on endless conversations about my famous great-grandmother, Lucinda Macklin.

Over a hundred years ago, Lucinda was a kitchen servant in Tennessee's Old South. I was told in no uncertain terms that a "house slave" had higher status than a "field slave." But the highest rank in prestige and power went to the "head slave" in the kitchen. That was Lucinda's place and she ran it like a queen. The kitchen was the center of everything from food to news. The "head slave" had keys to every one of the rooms. It was sort of like Bell's kitchen in Alex Haley's *Roots*. Lucinda was right in the center of all plantation activity and was always one of the first to learn news of the North and other topics of interest. Of course all of this was passed on to the children, who were inevitably underfoot in the kitchen. Grandmother Ausiebelle was one of those kids. She passed on all she knew to my mother, who in turn passed it on to me. I took fierce pride in my family history and our contributions to black culinary artistry.

Spices grew wild in the South and were creatively employed by the imaginative black women who worked in the kitchen. Slave women took advantage of the rich supply of fruits, grains, and game to adapt their old recipes or invent new ones, in combination with their special secrets of meat preservation brought from Africa.

Great-grandmother Lucinda created her own barbecue sauce. She developed a tangy sauce with diverse herbs and spices to marinate and tenderize beef, poultry, or fish before cooking it. Lucinda's authentic barbecue sauce made her a local celebrity.

After the close of the Civil War, Lucinda sold land she'd acquired to a famous educator named Issac Lane. He opened a liberal arts college for black students in Jackson, Tennessee, and implored Lucinda to come and be head cook.

Lucinda spent the next twenty-four years teaching anyone who wanted to learn the secrets of real Southern cuisine and in doing so, my great-grandmother became a celebrity at Lane College.

Grandma Ausiebelle followed in her mother's footsteps, except that she moved north in search of a better life. She found a job in the finest country club in Peoria, Illinois. She also found a husband, another gourmet cook. It wasn't long before my mother, Thelma, was born and soon followed right along in the family tradition.

Mom and Grandma often worked together in such notable spots as the Sheraton, Blackstone, and Drake hotels in Chicago. By the time I came along, my mother was a private cook for wealthy and famous families in the Chicago area. My apprenticeship began early. As soon as I was able to stand on a stool and reach the countertop, I started chopping herbs and preparing meats for barbecue.

These strong women taught me to be proud of our culinary history and our contributions to American cuisine. They also emphasized that a good black gourmet cook could always find a job.

When World War II began, I was sent to live with relatives in Tennessee. This firsthand farm experience was a real education to me. I learned to butcher hogs, grind the meat, and preserve it with sage wrapped in cheesecloth. I picked berries and made fresh preserves, milked goats and cows, and learned how to kill chickens. I also learned how to take ordinary vegetables like black-eyed peas, okra, tomatoes, and green beans and turn them into culinary delicacies any gourmet cook would serve with pride.

I have to smile when I hear men talk about their new freedom to respect strong women and deal with them as equals. I never knew there were any other choices. Ausiebelle is still very much alive in my memory. She was a strong, positive person. She was a force who took no nonsense from anyone. She was also very wise.

As a young man, I worked in bakeries, steel mills, and hotels. But I am a dreamer by nature and being surrounded by all the culture, knowledge, and wealth around Lake Michigan ignited my desire for a better life. I joined the service and got lucky: I met and married my wife, Linda. And just for the record, I did all the cooking. Economical dishes were my specialty.

A move to Shreveport, Louisiana, brought the delight of Creole cooking into our home. For me it was a sort of homecoming, with the smells of okra, crayfish, and varieties of gumbo reminding me of my roots.

After completing school and the service, I settled in San Diego. All my friends pleaded with me to bring my barbecue to any social function. But it was my mother who really threw me a curve; I shouldn't have been surprised. She traveled three thousand miles to spend twenty-four hours just to deliver one message: I had an obligation to history to keep the black culinary tradition alive, therefore I was to open a restaurant immediately. I did exactly as I was told.

LaMont's Authentic Barbecue opened its doors in Encinitas, California. Another one soon followed. The success of the restaurants and praise from food critics made me realize that people loved traditional black fare. They loved my food! I soon became the guest chef on "PM Magazine," and a line of products sporting my name appeared in stores like Neiman-Marcus, Bullock's, and Macy's. The response has been very gratifying, and not merely just for me.

There is a wealth of culinary history from black cooks that has been virtually ignored. Americans still chase after the illusion that French or Continental cuisine represents us. We have a rich history of authentic Southern cuisine that has belonged to us since the founding of America. These dishes can be prepared in our own homes. Down-home black food has always been here and always will be. Black food is a way of communicating family togetherness after a hard day's work. Dinnertime is for cementing family ties.

Americans should take pride that these shared cooking secrets have been passed down throughout the years by "the little people." I don't just mean my own family. I'm talking about sisters in the church, country bake sales where family pies won prizes, or the legions of families who handed down their special cooking skills by telling, not writing, their favorite recipes to family members.

I have specifically designed this book for all cooks to participate in these wonderful dishes which have been enjoyed for generations. This book is written so you can add your own "pinch" or "taste" to satisfy the palate of family or friends.

The recipes have been presented as simply and concisely as possible. The short introduction to each chapter is simply to inform you how and why these dishes came about. I think you'll find these glimpses of history fascinating. You should find pleasure in the recipes, which offer the delights of fine food and good eating.

And finally, this book is a sort of love letter to Lucinda, Ausiebelle, Thelma, and generations of courageous, creative black women whose unique culinary contributions must not be forgotten.

I guess this is my way of making sure.

LaMont Burns

Encinitas, CA
4-30-85

DOWN HOME
SOUTHERN COOKING

Chapter 1
BEVERAGES

It's funny, but the hot Santa Ana winds that blow through Southern California seem cool to me compared to the muggy, steaming heat of my childhood. Hot days go along with singing birds, gentle breezes, and frosty beverages prepared by Ausiebelle or my mother.

If I think about it real hard, I can recall the tastes and smells of special treats like my mother's syllabub mint tea or Ausiebelle's famous mint julep—minus the alcohol for me. They tasted wonderful, all icy and cool. I can remember how special I felt when Thelma or Ausiebelle would offer to "whip up something afreshing" for me. Little did I know that I was being shown the basics of Southern hospitality.

Here are some of Thelma and Ausiebelle's welcoming beverages. I've included my wife's spiced cider because it's flat-out delicious.

MINT JULEP

In the Deep South where the sun shines brighter, breezes are gentler, birds sing sweeter, the beverages are tastier. Long considered a plantation drink, the mint julep is distinctive in character.

What is more welcome, on a hot, muggy day than to be regaled with an icy beverage, cool in color and frost-dripping? That's what Southern hospitality is all about.

2 sprigs mint

1 tablespoon sugar

1/3 glass brandy

Shaved ice

Use a thin tumbler, very dry and warm. Break main veins on back of mint sprigs and put them into the tumbler. Add the sugar and fill the glass 1/3 full of brandy. Stir well until the sugar is dissolved. Fill the tumbler with shaved ice.

Place in the refrigerator 10–15 minutes. Serve when tumbler has frosted over on the outside.

This can be improved by shaking a little rum over the top of the ice just before serving. Be careful to handle so as not to disturb ice.

ORANGE JULEP

4 cups (1 quart) orange juice

1 cup sugar

Juice of 6 limes

1/2 cup mint leaves, minced

Crushed ice

2 cups (1 pint) seltzer

Mint sprigs for garnish

Mix orange juice, sugar, lime juice, and mint. Refrigerate for 1 hour.

Half-fill six glasses with ice. Fill glasses with equal proportion of prepared juice and seltzer.

Decorate edge of each glass with a sprig of mint. Serve cold.

PLANTER'S PUNCH

SERVES 4

1 tablespoon sugar

6 ounces Jamaica rum

3 ounces fine brandy

Juice of 1/2 lemon

1/2 cup pineapple juice

Shaved ice

Combine sugar, rum, and brandy in a tall glass. Add lemon and pineapple juices. Fill the glasses with shaved ice and chill before serving.

THELMA'S SYLLABUB

SERVES 4–6

The word "syllabub" is used in the South for any dish made with wine or cider and cream or milk which then becomes a curd to be sweetened, like a custard.

Whenever I asked my mother what syllabub was, she would simply answer, "It's a drink." Southern families have created their own versions of syllabub for decades. Because it is spicy, smooth, and sweet, syllabub is often a family favorite for special occasions. This is my mother's recipe for syllabub, a real highlight of my childhood and that of others whose mothers had their own recipe. Here is Thelma's.

1/2 cup fresh milk

1/2 cup hard cider

1/2 teaspoon vanilla

1/2 cup sugar

2 cups (1 pint) day-old whipping cream

Dash of nutmeg

Mix all the ingredients in a pitcher, except for the cream and nutmeg. Beat cream lightly and add to pitcher. Sprinkle with nutmeg. Chill.

Brandy can be used instead of cider. 1 tablespoon of sherry can be added, if desired.

LINDA'S SPECIAL CIDER

SERVES 6

4 cups (1 quart) sweet cider

1/4 cup sugar

12 whole cloves

8 whole allspice, cracked

Pinch of salt

6 sticks cinnamon

Mix all the ingredients in a saucepan and heat to the boiling point. Remove from heat and let stand for several hours, covered.

Remove cinnamon sticks and place in 6 individual cider mugs. Strain contents of saucepan through a sieve.

Reheat cider and pour into mugs. Stir with cinnamon sticks. Serve with freshly fried doughnuts.

ICED MINT TEA

SERVES 6

Mint Syrup:

1/2 cup water

2 cups sugar

Rind of 1 orange, grated

4–5 sprigs mint

Combine the water, sugar, and orange rind. Boil 5 minutes. Remove from heat, crush the mint leaves, and add. Let cool.

4 cups strongly brewed tea

Juice of 6 oranges

Crushed ice

6 slices orange

To the brewed tea add the orange juice. Sweeten with the cooled mint syrup. Divide the tea among 6 glasses half full of crushed ice and garnish each with a slice of orange. Serve immediately.

LOAFIN' COCKTAIL

SERVES 1

4 parts gin

1 part Italian vermouth

1 part grapefruit juice

Combine all ingredients in tall glass. Stir. Do not shake.

SAZERAC COCKTAIL

SERVES 1

1/3 ounce Bacardi rum

1/3 ounce rye whisky

1/6 ounce anisette

1/6 ounce dark rum

1 dash angostura bitters

1 dash orange bitters

3 dashes Pernod

Put all the ingredients into a cocktail shaker with some cracked ice. Shake well, strain, pour into glass. Serve.

SOUTHERN TOM AND JERRY

SERVES 6

12 eggs, well beaten

1 cup confectioner's sugar

6 jiggers bourbon

6 cups boiling water

Combine beaten eggs and sugar until thick. Line up six glasses and add a jigger of whiskey to each. Pour 2/3 cup of boiling water into each glass. Add a couple of spoonfuls of egg mixture to the top of each.

Garnish with a dash of nutmeg. Serve hot.

QUICK EGGNOG

6 eggs

1/4 cup sugar

3/4 cup heavy cream

1/2 teaspoon vanilla

6 cups cold milk

Dash of nutmeg

OPTIONAL:

4 ounces Jamaica rum

4 ounces brandy

Separate the eggs and beat the yolks with the sugar until thick and light in color. Beat the egg whites until they form soft peaks. Combine yolks and whites, stirring gently. Whip the cream and add vanilla. Add whipped cream and milk to eggs and stir gently. Add rum and brandy.

Put into chilled punch bowl and sprinkle with nutmeg. Cover and refrigerate until time to serve.

Chapter 2
APPETIZERS

It was Ausiebelle who first told me what appetizers were for. She said they were tasty morsels, bits and pieces of food to tempt the appetite for the big meal. She took great pride in her dinners, so no one got to wolf them down because they were starving. She told me that the secret to good appetizers was to serve just enough to keep stomachs from growling, but not enough to spoil the meal. She made it sound like a game—which, to my great surprise, years later she confessed was exactly how she regarded her quantity and timing of appetizers.

Always practical, Ausiebelle wanted everyone out of her kitchen while she prepared her secret treats. She loved the idea of surprising guests with previews of her culinary skills because she knew she'd knock them out with the meal.

My mother was like-minded. Appetizers were delicious delights with a purpose. "Feed your guests enough, but not too much. And above all, make those appetizers tempting without stealing thunder from the meal. Keep people cared for and catered to so you can keep them outa my kitchen!"

Here are some of the favorites Thelma and Ausiebelle passed on to me with their singular wisdom.

LOUISIANA MOLDED CRABMEAT

4 cups crabmeat, cooked and cleaned

Salt and pepper to taste

1/4 teaspoon mace

1/4 teaspoon coriander

1/4 cup butter

1 clove garlic, minced

30 crackers or toasted bread

Run the crabmeat through a meat grinder, or process briefly. Heat crabmeat in saucepan with salt, pepper, mace, and coriander. Melt butter with garlic and add to crabmeat.

Spoon into medium-size loaf pan mold. Press down firmly with the back of a spoon. Refrigerate for 1 hour or more.

When cold, remove by dipping mold in hot water to loosen crabmeat mixture. Turn out onto serving platter. Serve with crackers or toasted bread.

SHRIMP AND AVOCADO COCKTAIL

1/2 pound shrimp, cooked, shelled, and deveined

1 avocado

2 tablespoons mayonnaise

1 tablespoon catsup

1 tablespoon finely chopped fresh tomato

1 tablespoon finely chopped green pepper

1 tablespoon chili sauce

1/4 cup chopped black olives

Cut shrimp into bite-size pieces. Peel avocado and remove stone. Cut avocado into bite-size pieces. Mix all ingredients together, except for the black olives. Chill until time to serve.

Spoon into 4 to 6 cocktail dishes. Sprinkle with the olives and serve.

AVOCADO CANAPÉS

SERVES 4

12 slices sourdough bread

1/2 cup (1 stick) butter, softened

1 avocado

1 tablespoon grated onion

1 tablespoon lemon juice

Dash of cayenne pepper

Salt and pepper to taste

Mayonnaise

6 stuffed olives, halved

Parsley sprigs

Cut bread into doughnut-size rounds and toast on both sides. Spread with softened butter. Peel and stone avocado and mash with a fork.

Add onion, lemon juice, cayenne pepper, salt, pepper and just enough mayonnaise to make it of a spreading consistency.

Spread avocado mixture on toasted bread, rounding spread so it covers all of top and makes a small hill. Press half an olive into hill just before serving.

Arrange on serving platter with sprigs of parsley.

PAPAYA COCKTAIL

SERVES 4–6

2 ripe papayas

Juice of 1 lime

1 teaspoon sugar

1/4 teaspoon salt

6 sprigs mint

Cut out papaya balls with a melon baller, and place them in sherbet glasses.

Mix lime juice, sugar, and salt and pour over papaya balls. Add a sprig of mint to each glass. Chill and serve.

WELSH RAREBIT

SERVES 4–6

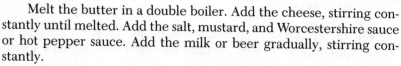

3 tablespoons butter

1 pound mild cheese, cubed

1/2 teaspoon salt

1/2 teaspoon mustard

1 teaspoon Worcestershire sauce or hot pepper sauce

1/2 cup milk or beer, heated

2 eggs, slightly beaten

4–6 slices buttered toast

Parsley sprigs

Melt the butter in a double boiler. Add the cheese, stirring constantly until melted. Add the salt, mustard, and Worcestershire sauce or hot pepper sauce. Add the milk or beer gradually, stirring constantly.

Add the eggs and stir until mixture becomes thick. Serve immediately on hot buttered toast. Garnish with parsley sprigs.

PIGS IN A BLANKET

SERVES 12

12 large oysters

1/2 teaspoon salt

Pinch of black pepper

1 (3-ounce) jar pimento

12 slices of bacon

Pinch of cayenne pepper

Season oysters with salt and pepper. Slice pimento into 12 strips and place one piece on each oyster. Wrap each oyster with slice of bacon. Pin with toothpick.

Broil for about 8 minutes, turning as many times as necessary to brown to a golden crisp. Sprinkle with cayenne pepper and serve hot.

ATLANTA APPETIZERS

1¹/2 tablespoons onion juice

2 tablespoons hot pepper sauce

2 (8-ounce) packages cream cheese

¹/2 pound dried beef, freshly sliced or packaged

10–12 gherkin pickles

Parsley sprigs

Blend onion juice and hot pepper sauce into cream cheese. Roll into walnut-size balls.

Cut dried beef into strips. Place a cheese ball at the end of each strip and roll it up, tucking in the edges as it is rolled. Fasten with a toothpick. Add a small gherkin to toothpick.

Chill. Serve on tray decorated with parsley.

CHEESE APPETIZERS

SERVES 4

2 egg whites

1 cup cheddar cheese (grated)

Dash of cayenne pepper

¹/4 cup stale fine bread crumbs

Vegetable oil for deep frying

2 cups (1 pint) sour cream

Beat egg whites until stiff. Add cheese, cayenne pepper, and bread crumbs. Mold into walnut-size balls. Let set for an hour or two.

Heat oil to 500° F.

Deep-fry until brown. Drain cheese balls on paper towels.

Serve with a bowl of sour cream as a dip.

Chapter 3
SOUPS, STEWS, POTLIKKERS, GUMBOS

I grew up believing that everybody ate the main meal of the day between two and three in the afternoon. That's how it was in the South, as well as in western Europe and with us, so I just assumed that's how it was with everyone. I also grew up believing in a code of dishes that had to be served in a certain order. Mom and Ausiebelle confirmed it as truth, so I bought it hook, line, and sinker.

You broke your fast with soup because warm liquids warm up the insides and prepare the body for digesting foods. Naturally you only served one dish at a time.

These soups, stews, or potlikkers were carefully prepared to make hearty, healthy broths and nutritional vegetables. Often they were the meal, except for Sunday when they began the meal. For that great day a dash of "shiny" (moonshine) would be tossed in to add a special touch to the start of a meal.

You can still find many of these popular soups like beef-okra and friar's chicken soup in little down-home family restaurants in the South.

It's interesting how many diet-conscious Americans have found that hearty soups do make an adequate meal. I can see Thelma and Ausiebelle just clucking at this tidbit of information as if it were news. They'd shake their heads to each other and simply smile that grin implying patience from those in the know with those who are learning.

Here are some of their special recipes to help speed up the process.

POT LIKKER

An absolute rule of thumb which existed in the South must have been the same everywhere in the founding of this country.

Don't throw anything away!

That meant you were a waster, and that was not a compliment. You saved everything because another use for it was bound to pop up.

Pot likker is probably the most accurate example of this from the South. Pot likker consisted of the water in which anything was cooked. Most frequently it was turnip greens. While the turnip greens were cooking to their final softness, you added anything you could find to cook along with them—preferably a ham bone.

This broth was called pot likker and it made many a meal served with cornmeal dodgers.

CORNMEAL DODGERS FOR POT LIKKER
SERVES 4

Vegetable greens such as turnip greens

1/2 teaspoon salt

1 cup white cornmeal

2 tablespoons melted butter

Cold water

Make the pot likker by cooking the greens in water to cover.

In a bowl, add salt to cornmeal and stir in the melted butter. Add sufficient cold water so the dough will hold its shape.

Mold dough into biscuit-size pieces and drop into boiling pot likker. Cook in closely covered pot for 20 minutes.

Serve cornmeal dodgers with the greens and the pot likker.

BURGOO
SERVES 6

Originally, burgoo was made from wild vegetables and animals found in the woods of the South. Today, meat from any domestic beast or barnyard fowl may be used along with any garden vegetables desired.

Combine in large stewing kettle the meat cut into 1-inch cubes, bones, dried beans, and dried or long-cooking vegetables such as onions, garlic, tomatoes, carrots, greens, ears of corn, celery, herbs, etc. Fill the kettle half full of water and bring to a slow boil.

Prepare the other vegetables to be used, such as potatoes, peas, string beans, etc., which need to be added 1/2 hour before cooking is completed.

Simmer until meat or fowl is fork-tender. Add salt and pepper to taste.

Serve Burgoo with pot likker on the side as a clear broth.

SOUTHERN BEAN SOUP   SERVES 6

1 cup dried beans

1 ham bone

3 tablespoons ham or bacon fat

1 cup chopped celery, including leaves

2 slices of onion, minced

6 cups cold water

2 tablespoons melted butter

3 tablespoons flour

Salt and pepper to taste

1 teaspoon lemon juice

Soak the beans in water to more than cover for at least 6 hours or overnight. Drain the beans and discard the water.

Combine the ham bone, ham or bacon fat, celery, onions, and the 6 cups water with the beans. Simmer gently until beans are tender. This timing depends on the kind of beans used.

Press through a strainer. Add enough water to make 5 cups.

Melt the butter in a saucepan, add flour, and cook until flour is browned. Add the salt, pepper, and lemon juice. Add small amount of strained bean mixture and cook, stirring constantly, until thickened. Add remaining beans and mix well. Reheat.

Serve very hot.

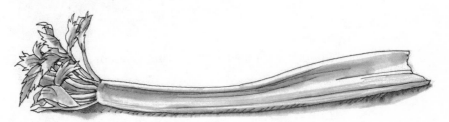

BLACK BEAN SOUP

SERVES 8–10

2 cups black beans

12 cups water

1/4 pound salt pork, cubed

1 carrot, chopped

3 cloves

1/4 teaspoon mace

3 small onions, chopped

Dash of red pepper

1/2 pound lean boiled beef, cut into small pieces

3 hard-boiled eggs, sliced

1 lemon, sliced thin

1 wineglass of sherry

Wash and pick over beans and soak overnight in water to more than cover.

Drain the beans and add the 12 cups of water. Add salt pork, carrots, cloves, mace, onions, and red pepper. Cover and simmer 4 hours or until beans are tender.*

Rub through a sieve and place in a soup tureen. Keep hot until time to serve. Just before serving, add the beef, sliced eggs, lemon, and sherry.

* To test beans for doneness, take a few beans out of the kettle with a slotted spoon and blow on them. If skins peel back, the beans are cooked.

OKRA SOUP

SERVES 6

1 soupbone

4 cups chopped okra

2 cups chopped tomatoes

2 tablespoons chives

Dash of ground ginger

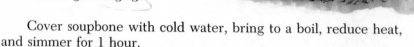

Cover soupbone with cold water, bring to a boil, reduce heat, and simmer for 1 hour.

Add okra and tomatoes. Simmer 3 hours or until thick.

Garnish with chives and ginger.

ALMOND CHICKEN SOUP

SERVES 8

3 cups chicken broth

1 teaspoon grated onion

1 bay leaf

Salt and pepper to taste

2 cups milk

1/2 cup almond meal

1 tablespoon flour

2 tablespoons butter, melted

1 cup heavy cream, whipped

Heat chicken broth, grated onion, bay leaf, salt, pepper, milk, and half of the almond meal over moderate heat.

Mix the flour with melted butter. Add small portion of milk and whip to eliminate lumps. Add to chicken broth mixture and heat, but don't boil. Remove bay leaf.

Serve in bouillon cups with a spoonful of whipped cream on top. Garnish with the remaining almond meal.

MARYLAND CREAM OF CRAB SOUP

SERVES 6

2 tablespoons butter

1 tablespoon flour

2 quarts milk

1/2 onion, grated

1 sprig parsley, chopped

1/4 cup chopped celery

Salt and pepper to taste

2 cups crabmeat

1 cup heavy cream (optional)

Melt butter in saucepan, add flour, and mix thoroughly. Gradually add the milk, stirring constantly until thickened. Add onions, parsley, celery, salt, and pepper. Simmer until soup thickens. Pick over crabmeat, discarding any shells. Add crabmeat.

Serve in individual bowls with a spoonful of cream on top.

DIAMONDBACK TERRAPIN STEW

3 large terrapins

6 hard-boiled eggs

1 onion, chopped

2 stalks celery, chopped

1 lemon (juice and grated rind)

1/2 teaspoon grated nutmeg

Pinch of cayenne pepper, salt, rosemary, thyme, and bay leaf

3 tablespoons flour

1/2 cup light cream

2 cups sherry

1/4 cup butter

Hot milk (if needed)

Buttered toast

Drop the live terrapins into boiling water. As soon as water boils again, turn off heat and let stand 5 minutes. Remove from water. With a towel rub the skin off the feet, tail, and head. Draw head out of shell with a skewer. Clip off the claws. Scrub the shells with boiling water. Break shells apart with sharp cleaver.

Remove the meat and liver. Discard gallbladder, heart, sandbag, and entrails. Cut liver into thin slices. Take out the terrapin eggs and remove membrane. Put the eggs in cold water and set aside.

Simmer meat, in water to cover, 15 minutes or until meat separates from bones. Discard bones.

Separate the whites from the yolks of the hard-boiled eggs and chop whites. Combine in soup kettle the yolks, onions, celery, lemon, nutmeg, cayenne pepper, salt, rosemary, thyme, and bay leaf, terrapin eggs, meat, and terrapin stock.

Simmer 1/2 hour. Remove bay leaf. Mix flour with equal amount of cold water and stir into stew.

Add cream, sherry, chopped egg whites, and butter. Heat again but don't boil. Add hot milk if stew becomes too thick.

Serve in chafing dish with buttered toast.

THELMA'S CREOLE BEEF STEW

1 1/2 pounds lean beef in 1 piece

1 garlic clove, pressed

3 tomatoes, chopped

1 large onion, chopped

1 green pepper, chopped

1 cup cut string beans

3 ears of corn, cut into 2-inch pieces

2 carrots, sliced

Salt and pepper to taste

1/4 teaspoon dried basil

1/4 teaspoon chopped fresh chives

1 teaspoon chopped parsley

1/4 teaspoon sage

3 potatoes, peeled and diced

2 tablespoons flour

Preheat oven to 350° F.

Place the beef in a deep iron kettle or Dutch oven. Arrange around beef the garlic, tomatoes, onions, green peppers, string beans, corn, carrots, salt and pepper, basil, chives, parsley, and sage. Barely cover with water and bake, covered, for 3 hours or until meat is fork-tender. Add more water if necessary to prevent drying out.

Add the potatoes the last half hour.

Remove meat from baking pan and place on serving platter. Arrange vegetables around meat.

Mix flour with 2 tablespoons of water and add to the meat juices. Stir constantly until thickened. Pour gravy over meat and serve.

BRUNSWICK STEW

1 (2–2¹/2-pound) frying chicken

3 tablespoons bacon fat

2 onions, chopped

3 cups water

3 tomatoes, peeled, quartered

¹/2 cup sherry

2 teaspoons hot pepper sauce

1 pound fresh lima beans

¹/2 cup sliced okra

3 ears of corn kernels cut from cob

2 tablespoons butter

Salt and pepper to taste

¹/4 teaspoon chopped parsley

¹/4 teaspoon oregano

1 garlic clove, minced

¹/4 teaspoon chopped fresh chives

¹/4 teaspoon dill seeds

¹/2 cup bread crumbs

Using a Dutch oven, brown the chicken on all sides in the bacon fat. Remove chicken and sauté onions. Return chicken to Dutch oven and add the water, tomatoes, sherry, and hot pepper sauce. Cover.

Cook slowly over low heat for ¹/2 hour. Shell lima beans and add with okra and corn. Simmer 1 hour.

Add butter, salt, pepper, parsley, oregano, garlic, chives, dill seeds, and bread crumbs. Simmer ¹/2 hour longer.

OYSTER STEW

- 2 cups oysters
- 4 cups (1 quart) milk
- 2 tablespoons butter
- 1 tablespoon finely chopped parsley
- Dash of onion juice
- Salt and pepper to taste
- Oyster crackers

Put oysters, in their own juices, into a saucepan. Heat slowly until edges of oysters begin to curl. Be careful not to overcook, this should take only a minute or two. Shake pan carefully so as not to break oysters.

Add milk, butter, parsley, onion juice, salt, and pepper.

Serve in heated soup bowls, with oyster crackers.

CHICKEN GUMBO

- 1 (2–2¹/₂-pound) chicken
- 3 tablespoons flour
- 3 tablespoons butter
- 1 teaspoon sugar
- 1/2 sweet red pepper, chopped
- 4 cups cut okra
- 1 large can tomatoes or 5–6 ripe tomatoes, skinned
- 1 can corn or niblets or kernels cut from 3 ears of fresh corn
- 2 sprigs parsley, chopped
- 2 basil leaves, snipped

Simmer chicken in water to cover for 1 hour. Remove chicken from stock and cool. Skin chicken and pick meat from bones. Cut chicken into bite-size pieces.

Brown the flour in the butter, add sugar, vegetables, and chicken stock. Simmer until vegetables are tender and the gumbo is thick.

Add the cooked and cut chicken and serve hot.

THELMA'S CRAYFISH BISQUE

2 dozen crayfish

4 cups (1 quart) boiling water

2 stalks celery

2 sprigs parsley, chopped

1/4 teaspoon thyme

1/4 teaspoon rosemary

2 carrots, scraped

2 onions, peeled

6 tablespoons cracker crumbs

1/4 cup milk

3 tablespoons butter

2 tablespoons flour

Salt and pepper to taste

1 egg, well beaten

Soak crayfish in cold water to cover for 30 minutes, then wash thoroughly, using a brush to remove dirt.

Put the crayfish in a pot with the boiling water, the celery, half of the parsley, half of the thyme, half of the rosemary, the carrots, and 1 onion and simmer 25 minutes. Strain, discard vegetables, and reserve the cooking water. Pick the meat from the crayfish heads and bodies. Set aside the heads.

Moisten cracker crumbs with the milk. Finely chop the crayfish meat and add to the cracker crumbs. Chop the other onion and sauté in 1 tablespoon of the butter. Add 1 tablespoon of the flour, 1 tablespoon of the crayfish broth, the remaining parsley, thyme, rosemary, and salt and pepper.

Sauté about 2 minutes. Add crayfish mixture and cook 2–3 minutes longer. Remove from heat and let cool slightly. Add egg and mix thoroughly.

Fill crayfish heads with the cracker mixture. Dredge the heads in flour and fry in butter until golden brown. Drain on paper towels or crumpled paper. Set aside in warm place while making the bisque.

Bisque:

Heat water in which crayfish and vegetables were boiled. Add remaining tablespoon of flour combined with 2 tablespoons water and stir until thickened. Simmer for 12 minutes. Just before serving, add the stuffed crayfish heads. Serve hot.

SHRIMP GUMBO   SERVES 10–12

8 cups fresh shrimp

3 onions

1/2 cup vinegar

Pinch of salt

2 quarts water

6 large tomatoes, chopped

2 bay leaves

4 cups sliced okra

Sprig each of parsley and thyme

1 tablespoon hot pepper sauce

1 sweet red pepper, chopped

Pinch of sugar

1 tablespoon butter

2 tablespoons flour

1 cup cooked rice

Simmer the shrimp with 2 of the onions, chopped, the vinegar, and a pinch of salt in the 2 quarts of water until shrimp turn pink. Do not overcook; this takes but a minute or two after water returns to a boil. Drain, saving water to make the gumbo. Peel and devein shrimp, discarding the shells. If using large shrimp, cut into bite-size pieces.

Add tomatoes, bay leaves, okra, parsley, thyme, hot pepper sauce, red pepper, and sugar to the shrimp water. Simmer 1 hour in covered kettle. Remove bay leaves.

Chop remaining onion and sauté in butter; add flour and blend together. Add some of the liquid from the gumbo and stir until smooth, then add to gumbo pot. Add shrimp and rice and mix gently.

Serve with heavy-crusted bread.

CHICKEN OYSTER GUMBO

1 (2–2½-pound) chicken, sectioned into 8 pieces

1 pound stew beef

1 cup sliced okra

1 onion, chopped

6 cups cold water

1 tablespoon butter

2 dozen oysters

Salt and pepper

½ tablespoon ground sassafras leaves or filé

In a covered pot, simmer the chicken, beef, okra, onions, and water 1½–2 hours or until meat is fork-tender.

Remove chicken and meat and cool enough to handle. Pick over the chicken and discard the bones. Cut chicken and meat into bite-size pieces and return to liquid.

Melt butter and sauté oysters (including liquid) until edges curl. Add to pot. Add salt and pepper to taste, and sassafras or filé. Stir until thickened.

Serve gumbo in soup bowls.

Chapter 4
FRITTERS, PANCAKES, MUSH, WAFFLES

Childhood memories are always selective, but most of my favorites center around the morning, with everyone up and about and busy. I was blessed with a mother and grandmother who greeted each day with a smile and a sense of something new. When I would stumble into the kitchen, one of them would invariably read off the menu of available breakfast treats, each one as delicious as the last.

I grew up on fritters, pancakes, mush, and waffles. Half of the fun was watching them being prepared—the sizzle of hot grease in the pan and the agile hands that flipped and turned whatever was cooking.

I was king of the kitchen at breakfast time. There was always a variety to choose from, but most importantly there was always someone who loved me waiting to fix it for me.

Here are some dishes that will always be special to me. Even their smell triggers memories within me of two ladies who always made my day. These recipes are all surefire Southern in flavor and originality. Imagine the "Old Mammy" with her head tied in a red bandana stirring and tasting her cornmeal mush. And who but the Southerner has stuck so tenaciously to hominy as a way of life?

Sour Milk Griddle Cakes are a delight, and they too uphold the Southern tradition of good eating. Corn was a staple, so what is more natural than Corn Bread Fritters, Cornmeal Dodgers, and Virginia Waffles? Enjoy.

FLANNEL CAKES

2 cups flour

2 teaspoons sugar

3 teaspoons baking powder

1/2 teaspoon salt

2 eggs, separated

1 1/2 cups milk

2 tablespoons melted butter

Syrup for serving

Sift together flour, sugar, baking powder, and salt. Beat egg yolks and add to the milk. Pour into the flour. Add the melted butter. Beat egg whites well and add to the mixture.

Drop by the spoonful onto a greased hot griddle. When bubbles begin to form on the uncooked side, turn cakes and cook on the other side.

Serve with a syrup.

CORNMEAL MUSH

SERVES 4–6

1 cup yellow cornmeal

8 cups (2 quarts) boiling water

1 teaspoon salt

Maple syrup and sausage

Moisten cornmeal with just enough cold water to make it runny. Put the boiling water in the top part of a double boiler with the salt, and add the cornmeal slowly, stirring constantly.

Simmer over low heat, stirring frequently, for 1 hour.

Set pot into bottom part of double boiler half full of simmering water. Cook for 3 hours, taking care not to let double boiler go dry.

Pack into a well-greased bread pan and refrigerate until cold and firm.

Unmold on floured surface and cut into 1/2-inch strips. Roll in flour. Fry on greased griddle until golden brown on both sides.

Serve with maple syrup and sausage.

HOMINY GRITS

   1 cup hominy grits

   4 cups boiling water

   1 teaspoon salt

   1 tablespoon bacon fat

   Parsley, chopped

Pour hominy grits* into the boiling, salted water and stir until it returns to a boil. Lower the flame and let simmer for 1 hour, stirring frequently.

When ready to serve, add the bacon fat and stir well. Sprinkle with parsley.

* Hominy is parched corn that has been hulled. Hominy grits are dried hominy, coarsely ground to meal.

FRIED HOMINY

   1 cup hominy grits

   4 cups cold water

   1 teaspoon salt

   Pinch of sugar

   Egg Batter

Add the hominy grits to the water and stir until it comes to the boiling point. Add the salt and sugar. Lower heat and simmer for 1 hour, stirring frequently. Remove from heat and drain if there is any liquid. Pour into buttered bread pan. Refrigerate until cold and firm.

Unmold on floured surface and cut into 1/2-inch slices.

Egg Batter:

   1 egg

   1 tablespoon milk

   Flour for dredging

Beat together the egg and milk. Dredge each slice with flour, then dip in the egg mixture. Place on greased griddle. Fry until brown on both sides.

Good served with cranberry jelly, bacon, and stewed fruit.

CORN FRITTERS

    1 cup flour

    1 teaspoon baking powder

    1/2 teaspoon salt

    1 egg, well beaten

    1/4 cup milk

    1/2 tablespoon melted butter

    1 cup canned crushed corn, drained

    Lemon Sauce

Sift dry ingredients together. Gradually add the beaten egg and milk. Add butter and corn.

Drop by spoonfuls into hot deep fat and fry until well browned. Drain on paper towels. Serve with Lemon Sauce.

Lemon Sauce:

    1/2 cup sugar

    1 tablespoon cornstarch

    1 cup boiling water

    1 tablespoon melted butter

    Juice of 1/2 lemon

    Grated rind of lemon

Mix sugar and cornstarch in a saucepan. Stir in boiling water. Add butter, lemon juice, and rind. Boil and stir until mixture thickens.

Serve on Corn Fritters.

HOECAKES

    2 cups yellow cornmeal

    1/4 teaspoon salt

    1 cup boiling water or scalded milk

Moisten the cornmeal and salt with the boiling water or scalded milk. Allow to stand 1 hour to make a pancake-like mixture.

Drop 2–3 teaspoons of this batter on a hot, greased griddle.

Smooth it out to make a cake about 1/2 inch thick. Cook until brown on bottom. Turn it over and brown other side.

Serve very hot for breakfast, with sausages or bacon.

CORNMEAL DODGERS SERVES 4–6

1 1/2 cups cornmeal

4 1/2 cups water

3/4 cup flour

3 eggs, beaten

Bacon fat for frying

Maple syrup

Combine the cornmeal with the water in a saucepan and heat, stirring. When slightly thickened, remove from heat and add the flour. Add eggs.

Preheat griddle and grease with bacon fat. Drop 1 tablespoon of batter at a time on griddle. Brown on both sides.

Serve with maple syrup.

SOUR MILK GRIDDLE CAKES SERVES 4–6

1 1/2 cups flour

1 tablespoon sugar

1 teaspoon baking soda

1 cup sour milk or buttermilk

2 eggs

1 tablespoon melted butter

Powdered sugar for serving

Melted butter for serving

Sift the flour and sugar together. Dissolve the baking soda in the sour milk or buttermilk. Add to the flour. Drop in the unbeaten eggs and beat well. Add the 1 tablespoon of melted butter.

Drop by the spoonful onto a hot greased griddle and brown on both sides.

Sprinkle with the powdered sugar and serve with hot melted butter.

GEORGIA FLAPJACKS

SERVES 4–6

2 cups flour

11/2 teaspoons baking soda

1/2 teaspoon salt

1 tablespoon sugar

2 eggs, beaten

2 cups sour milk

11/2 tablespoons melted butter

Melted butter for serving

Maple syrup for serving

Sift flour. Add soda, salt, and sugar. Mix well and sift again. Mix eggs and sour milk and gradually add to flour mixture. Beat until smooth and free of lumps. Add the 11/2 tablespoons melted butter. Pour batter into pitcher.

Preheat griddle and grease with butter. Pour out enough batter to make a cake about 5 inches in diameter. Cook over moderate heat until porous and brown underneath. Turn and brown on the other side.

Serve with melted butter and maple syrup.

CORN BREAD FRITTERS

SERVES 4–6

1 cup cornmeal

1 cup flour

1/2 teaspoon salt

2 teaspoons baking powder

1 egg, beaten

11/2 cups milk

Fat or oil for frying

Mix together the cornmeal, flour, salt, and baking powder. Add the egg and enough of the milk to make a stiff batter.

Drop the batter from a spoon into deep hot fat and fry until golden brown, turning once. Drain fritters on paper towels.

Serve at breakfast or with soups.

RICE WAFFLES

2 eggs, separated

1 cup cooked rice

2 tablespoons melted butter

2 cups flour

3 teaspoons baking powder

1/2 teaspoon salt

Milk if needed

Soft butter for serving

Powdered sugar for serving

Beat the egg yolks. Add the rice, butter, flour, baking powder, and salt. Beat the egg whites until stiff and fold in. If needed, add enough milk to make a batter-like consistency.

Pour 1/4 cup of the batter into a preheated waffle iron and cook until golden brown.

Serve with soft butter and powdered sugar.

LOUISIANA WAFFLES

SERVES 4–6

3 eggs, separated

1 1/2 cups milk

2 cups flour

4 teaspoons baking powder

1/2 teaspoon salt

5 tablespoons melted butter

Melted butter for serving

Powdered sugar for serving

Beat the egg yolks and add the milk. Sift dry ingredients together and add to milk mixture. Add the melted butter. Beat the egg whites until stiff and fold into the first mixture.

Pour 1/4 cup of the batter into waffle iron and cook until golden brown.

Serve with melted butter and powdered sugar.

VIRGINIA WAFFLES

1/2 cup white cornmeal

11/2 cups boiling water

3 cups flour

3 tablespoons sugar

3 tablespoons baking powder

1/2 teaspoon salt

11/2 cups milk

2 eggs, separated

3 tablespoons melted butter

Whipped butter for serving

Brown sugar for serving

Gradually add the cornmeal to the boiling water, stirring constantly. Cook the mixture in top of double boiler for 30 minutes, stirring frequently.

Sift together the flour, sugar, baking powder, and salt.

Add the milk, sifted dry ingredients, well-beaten egg yolks, melted butter, and beaten egg whites to the cornmeal mixture. Put 1 tablespoon of mixture in the center of each section of a preheated waffle iron. Cook until waffle is well puffed and a delicate brown.

Serve with whipped butter and brown sugar.

40   DOWN HOME SOUTHERN COOKING

Chapter 5
EGGS, RICE, BEANS

E ggs, rice, and beans are the staples of down-home Southern cooking. Regardless of the economic climate, these basics have always been available to create delicious, nourishing meals. Today's vegetarians boast of the vitamins and minerals contained in these simple foods. My great-grandmother could have told you that, although she would not have spoken of proteins and carbohydrates. Her message would have been simply: "Eat this. It's good and good for you."

EGGS

"Everybody eats eggs," Ausiebelle used to say with her particular brand of certainty. I took her at her word, figuring that everybody in the world must have chickens, birds, or some kind of fowl that provided eggs. I'd be sent out to gather the eggs in a basket and I'd wonder if other kids all over the world were doing the same.

There were always fresh eggs for eating in any number of ways. I never believed that eggs were just a breakfast food. My mother and grandmother would make omelets, eggs with fancy sauces, and stuffed eggs for special occasions. They could whip up wonders from the contents of those shells.

Eggs are a versatile, healthful food. They are appropriate for any meal, any time of the day. They give the cook the opportunity to use his or her imagination and creativity, and to experiment with different sauces and herbs.

Ausiebelle was a real artist with eggs. They were like her own personal canvas. I learned not to ask her what she was doing until it was done. But it always turned out to be delicious. My mother had the same touch.

Here are some of my favorites, literally the fruits of my gathering.

Since everybody eats eggs, perhaps the following pages will show you some new ways to prepare them.

GOLDENROD EGGS BALTIMORE   SERVES 2

2 tablespoons butter

2 tablespoons flour

1 cup warm milk

Salt and pepper to taste

4 hard-boiled eggs

3 slices bread

Parsley for garnish

Melt butter, add flour, mixing thoroughly. Add warmed milk and stir constantly over moderate heat until smooth. Add salt and pepper.

Separate yolks and whites. Chop the whites fine and add to sauce. Make toast, remove crusts, and butter. Cut 1 slice of toast into

4 triangles. Put 1 whole slice of toast in middle of each serving dish and pour cream sauce mixture over it. Arrange 2 of the triangles beside each full slice. Mash yolks through a strainer over each serving. Garnish with parsley and serve.

To serve this dish hot it is necessary to work with speed, having everything ready at once. Or use heated ovenproof serving dishes.

NEW ORLEANS EGGS   SERVES 4–6

2 1/2 cups chopped tomatoes

1 small onion, chopped

1/2 green pepper, chopped

1/2 cup chopped celery

1 bay leaf

1/4 teaspoon salt

3/4 cup bread crumbs

Butter for casserole

4 eggs

Sprinkle of black pepper

1/2 cup grated sharp cheese

Preheat oven to 325° F.

Sauté the tomatoes, onions, green peppers, celery, bay leaf, and salt for 10 minutes.

Remove bay leaf. Add bread crumbs and place in buttered 1-quart casserole. Break eggs on top (don't break egg yolks). Sprinkle with the black pepper. Cover with the cheese.

Bake about 5 minutes, until eggs have set and cheese is bubbly. Serve immediately.

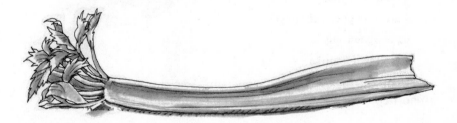

EGGS STUFFED
WITH CHICKEN LIVERS

SERVES 4

2 chicken livers

1/2 teaspoon onion juice

2 tablespoons butter

4 hard-boiled eggs

1 teaspoon chopped parsley

Salt and pepper to taste

Dash of hot pepper sauce

Butter for casserole

1/4 cup grated mild cheese

Parsley to decorate

Preheat oven to 375° F.

Clean the livers, chop fine, and sprinkle with the onion juice. Sauté in the butter.

Cut the eggs in half lengthwise, remove yolks and force them through a sieve. Add parsley, salt, pepper, and hot pepper sauce. Combine chicken livers and egg-yolk mixture and fill whites. Arrange stuffed egg halves in buttered 1-quart casserole. Sprinkle with the cheese.

Bake until cheese melts. Serve on canapé tray with sprigs of parsley decorating tray.

CREOLE OMELET

SERVES 4

Creole Sauce:

2 tablespoons peanut oil

2 onions, chopped

4 tomatoes, chopped

2 green peppers, chopped

1/2 teaspoon salt

1 teaspoon paprika

Heat the peanut oil in saucepan. Add the onions, tomatoes, green peppers, salt and paprika. Simmer until needed.

Omelet:

4 eggs

4 tablespoons water

1/2 teaspoon salt

1 tablespoon butter

Beat eggs in a bowl with the water and dash of salt. Heat butter in skillet until light brown. Add beaten eggs. Cook on low heat and as the edges of eggs firm, lift with a spatula and let the uncooked part run underneath.

When omelet is browned underneath and creamy on top, fold once and slip onto a hot plate. Surround omelet with Creole Sauce.

EGGS PONCE DE LEON   SERVES 6

6 hard-boiled eggs

1/2 onion, chopped

1/2 cup chopped celery

1/4 cup chopped green pepper

2 tablespoons butter

2 tablespoons flour

2 cups tomato juice

Salt and pepper to taste

1/2 cup tiny mushrooms

1/2 teaspoon hot pepper sauce

Butter for casserole

1/2 cup cracker or bread crumbs

Butter to dot top of casserole

Preheat oven to 375° F.

Chop the egg whites and mash the yolks and set aside. Sauté the onions, celery, and green peppers in the butter. Add the flour and mix in well. Add tomato juice, salt, and pepper. Simmer 10–15 minutes, stirring constantly until thickened. Mix in mushrooms and hot pepper sauce. Add the egg whites and yolks.

Pour into buttered 1-quart casserole. Sprinkle with cracker or bread crumbs. Dot with butter.

Bake 20 minutes or until golden brown. Serve hot.

RICE AND BEANS

It makes me smile to hear the new health-conscious experts extol the nutritious virtues of rice and beans. Ausiebelle would have told you as much in five seconds, then clucked that "any fool could figure that out." Beans and rice have always been staples in Southern cuisine. To Southern cooks the constant use of beans and rice did not imply bland dishes or repetitious menus.

There are many ingenious ways to prepare beans and rice as zesty, creative dishes. These nourishing, delicious recipes have been handed down in my family for generations. They are healthful dishes—easy on the cook and easy on the budget.

WILD RICE AND MUSHROOMS — SERVES 4–6

1 cup wild rice

2¹/2 cups boiling water

1 pound mushrooms, sliced

2 tablespoons butter

2 tablespoons flour

¹/2 teaspoon mustard

1 cup milk

Cover the rice with the boiling water and boil rapidly for 15 minutes or until water is absorbed. Turn off heat but let it steam until dry.

Sauté mushrooms in the butter until well browned. Remove mushrooms and set aside. Add the flour and mustard to butter and stir into a paste over moderate heat. Add the milk gradually and stir until smooth and free of lumps. Cook over moderate heat until thick, stirring constantly. Add cooked mushrooms.

Preheat oven to 375° F.

Pour rice into a 1- or 1¹/2-quart buttered casserole. Spread mushrooms over rice. Bake until golden brown.

RICE AND CHICKEN CASSEROLE   SERVES 8–10

1 (2½-pound) chicken

2 cups rice

2 tablespoons butter

2 cups milk

2 eggs, beaten

Boil the chicken 1 hour in water to half-cover the chicken. Remove chicken from liquid. Cool. Skin the chicken and pick meat from bones. Cut into bite-size pieces.

Cook rice according to package directions, using the broth from the boiled chicken instead of water. Stir in butter, milk, and eggs.

Preheat oven to 350° F.

Layer rice and chicken in 2-quart buttered casserole.

Bake ½ hour or until golden brown.

THELMA'S RICE CROQUETTES   SERVES 4–6

2½ cups cooked rice

1 cup grated cheddar cheese

½ cup melted butter

½ cup chopped pimento

1 tablespoon chopped onions

Pinch of salt, pepper, paprika, garlic powder

1 teaspoon baking powder

1 egg, beaten

½ cup bread crumbs

1 pound lard or 4 cups oil for deep frying

White Sauce

1 teaspoon chopped parsley

Mix well all the ingredients except the lard or frying oil. Mold into croquettes the size of golf balls. Drop into hot fat and fry until brown and crisp.

Serve with White Sauce (see Index) and garnish with chopped parsley.

MULATTO RICE

I had no idea what the name of this dish meant until my grand-mother explained it to me.

In the colonial days, white Southerners and black slaves both consumed a lot of rice as a main staple. Whites ate their rice steamed, with butter. Blacks preferred a heartier, spicier version made with tomatoes, chilies, and herbs. Bit by bit, tastes commingled. Black cooks would dress up the rice a little with their own touch. After the Civil War, Black women taught white women how to make a main dish out of rice by adding all the extra ingredients. This dish rapidly became known as Mulatto Rice. Here's Ausiebelle's version.

1/2 pound bacon

1 small onion, chopped

1 cup chopped tomatoes

2 cups cooked rice

Cut bacon into small pieces and fry until crisp. Remove bacon from skillet.

Sauté onions in bacon fat. Add tomatoes, cooked rice, and bacon bits. Blend well. Serve hot.

CURRIED RICE

2 cups rice, uncooked

1 green pepper, chopped

1 onion, chopped

2 cups chopped tomatoes

3 cups water

4 tablespoons melted butter

1 tablespoon curry powder

3 tablespoons flour

Parmesan cheese

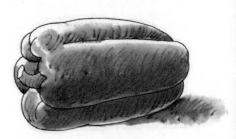

Preheat oven to 375° F.

Mix all ingredients except the Parmesan cheese. Put into a 1 1/2- to 2-quart buttered casserole. Sprinkle Parmesan cheese on top.

Bake for 1 hour or until onion and green pepper are thoroughly cooked and liquid has been absorbed.

Sprinkle with the cheese. Serve hot.

RICE AND PINEAPPLE CASSEROLE   SERVES 4–6

4 cups cooked rice

1 large can (12 ounces) sliced pineapple

1 cup brown sugar

1/2 teaspoon aniseed

Preheat oven to 350° F.

Put 1/2 inch layer of cooked rice in bottom of a buttered 1-quart casserole. Dot with butter. Place pineapple on rice. Sprinkle with some of the brown sugar and aniseed.

Repeat until all ingredients are used, with pineapple on top. Pour juice over top.

Bake for 30 minutes, or until all ingredients are bubbly hot. Serve hot.

CREOLE GOULASH   SERVES 6

1/2 pound sliced bacon

2 (1-pound) cans red kidney beans, drained

4 cups (1 quart) tomatoes

1 teaspoon baking powder

1/4 teaspoon oregano

1/4 teaspoon cumin seeds

1 teaspoon curry powder

1/4 pound sharp cheese, grated

Preheat oven to 350° F.

Fry the bacon until crisp. Remove bacon from pan and set aside. Add the beans to the bacon fat. Add tomatoes, baking powder, oregano, cumin seeds, and curry powder.

Put into 1¹/₂-quart greased casserole. Cover and bake for 1 hour.

Remove the cover and sprinkle with cheese. Arrange bacon over cheese and bake 10 minutes longer.

Serve in casserole.

Chapter 6
FRUITS AND VEGETABLES

Though I was very young at the time, I can remember this day as if it were yesterday. My mother was gathering spices and I was in the kitchen with grandmother Ausiebelle. She was preparing collard greens and held up a bunch for me to see. I realize now that this green bouquet was her chosen prop.

"Your great-grandmother, Lucinda, was a courageous Christian woman," she began. I had no idea where all this was leading. I'd heard the first part before. She raised her greens like a torch.

"What makes people great, LaMont, is their capacity to give unto others regardless of the circumstances." I nodded in agreement.

"What do you know about the Civil War?" she asked.

I told her all I knew from school, books, and things I'd heard. "We were slaves," I added for emphasis. She did not deny that reality. Lucinda had been a slave too. "The South lost and we got to be free." Still holding the collard greens, she smiled a wizened grin.

She asked me what I thought the South was like after the war.

"Black people must have been celebrating," I proudly answered.

"With what?"

"White people's food and wine."

She laughed out loud. "What food and wine? Everything was burned."

I hadn't known this. She told me the South had been destroyed. People were homeless and hungry, whites and slaves alike.

"They had to rely on what grew in the soil to survive. Like this," she said, holding up the collard greens again. "But white people had no idea what to do, or even what to pick that they could eat."

I knew better than to say serves 'em right. That was not a Christian attitude and Ausiebelle wouldn't have it.

"Your great-grandmother Lucinda, and others like her, showed them what to do.

"They taught white women to prepare collard greens, black-eyed peas, sassafras tea, watermelon pickles, okra and tomatoes, pot-likkers, burgoo, cornbread, and molasses."

"Why did they help them? Wasn't it like sharing secrets with the enemy?"

"They helped them because they were great women who knew it was the right thing to do. And they must never be forgotten. Someday you'll pass this story on too."

This chapter on vegetables and fruits is dedicated to those un-selfish women who followed their instincts of goodness instead of the bitter lessons of history. I feel very proud to count my great-grand-mother amongst them. This is my way of passing it on. I hope you will do the same.

SPICED CANTALOUPE
MAKES 5–6 1-POUND JARS

7 pounds cantaloupe

2 cups vinegar

2 cups water

3 pounds sugar

8 sticks cinnamon

8 whole cloves

Peel off rind and cut cantaloupes into 1-inch cubes. Soak overnight in vinegar and water.

In the morning, add sugar, cinnamon, and cloves. Bring to a rapid boil, then reduce heat and simmer 1 1/2 hours or until cantaloupe becomes almost transparent.

Place in clean, sterile* jars and seal.

* Sterilize jars by dipping into boiling hot water with tongs. Don't let anything touch insides of the jars after sterilizing, except the hot cantaloupe.

BAKED PAPAYA
SERVES 4–6

4 cups papaya pulp

1 cup coconut meat, shredded

1 orange (pulp, juice, and grated rind)

4 eggs

4 cups milk

1 cup sugar

Preheat oven to 350° F.

Arrange papaya, coconut, and orange in baking dish.

Make a custard by beating together the eggs, milk, and sugar. Pour over the papaya.

Bake until silver knife comes clean.*

* Insert knife in center of custard. If it comes out clean, it is done. If any of the milk clings to knife, bake longer.

SWEET POTATO PONE

SERVES 4

A "pone" (rhymes with phone) is similar to a biscuit or a doughnut. It is usually made from a vegetable, like a corn pone or, in this case, a sweet potato. Pones make an excellent side dish to a meal as well as a delightful treat in their own right. These are my mother's sweet potato pones. They were a childhood favorite, filling the kitchen with wonderful aromas that said, "Welcome."

1 cup sugar

1 cup butter, melted

2 cups raw sweet potato, grated

1/2 cup milk

1 teaspoon powdered ginger

Grated rind of 1 orange

Preheat oven to 350° F.

Blend the sugar and butter. Add grated sweet potato and milk. Beat well. Add ginger and orange rind.

Place in shallow baking dish. Bake until golden brown.

FRESH LIMA BEANS

SERVES 6–8

4 cups (1 quart) fresh lima beans

1 tablespoon bacon fat

1/2 teaspoon salt

2 tablespoons milk

2 tablespoons cream

2 strips of bacon, fried crisp

Wash and pick over the beans. Cover with boiling water. Add bacon fat and salt. Simmer 18 minutes. Raise the heat and boil quickly until water has almost completely evaporated. Add the milk and cream.

Remove from heat just as milk is about to boil. Add the crisp bacon pieces.

Serve hot.

STRING BEANS AND BACON

SERVES 6–8

2 cups cut string beans

2 medium potatoes, diced

1/4 pound bacon, diced, cooked crisp

1/4 teaspoon salt

Dash of pepper

1/4 teaspoon celery seed

1 cup water

1 small onion, chopped

Put all ingredients into a saucepan and simmer, covered, 15 minutes or until potatoes are tender.
Serve hot.

CORN PUDDING

SERVES 4–6

3 tablespoons yellow cornmeal

1 teaspoon salt

1/2 teaspoon paprika

1/2 cup cold milk

2 cups milk, scalded

1 tablespoon bacon fat

2 cups fresh corn kernels cut from cob

2 eggs, beaten

1/4 cup chopped green or red pepper, pimento, or parsley

Preheat oven to 350° F.

In top of double boiler, combine cornmeal, salt, paprika, and cold milk. Stir in scalded milk. Bring water in bottom of double boiler to boil. Insert top of double boiler and cook until mixture thickens, stirring frequently.

Remove from heat and stir in remaining ingredients. Pour into a buttered 1-quart casserole. Set casserole in a pan of warm water so that water comes halfway up the sides of the casserole.

Bake for 1 hour, or until center is firm to the touch of a finger.

SOUTHERN CORN CUSTARD

SERVES 4–6

3 eggs, beaten

2 cups cooked corn kernels

2 cups milk

2 tablespoons melted butter

Salt and pepper to taste

1/2 teaspoon sugar

Sprinkle of cracker crumbs

Butter for top

Preheat oven to 250° F.

To beaten eggs, add the corn. Add the milk and butter. Stir well. Add the salt, pepper, and sugar and mix well. Pour into well-buttered 1-quart casserole. Sprinkle with cracker crumbs and dot with butter.

Bake in slow oven for about 40 minutes until custard sets, or until a silver knife inserted in the center comes out clean.

CANDIED YAMS

SERVES 4–6

Enough cooked sweet potatoes or
  yams to fill a 1-quart casserole

Sprinkle of salt and pepper

Sprinkle of paprika

2 tablespoons brown sugar for each layer

1/4 cup butter or bacon fat at room temperature

Sprinkle of cinnamon

1/2 cup water

Preheat oven to 300° F.

Pare and cut potatoes in halves, lengthwise. Place close together in buttered casserole. Makes 2 or 3 layers. Sprinkle each layer with salt, pepper, paprika, and brown sugar. Dot with butter or bacon fat. Sprinkle with cinnamon. Add water. Cover and bake for 25 minutes or until golden brown. Serve hot.

HASH BROWN POTATOES

1/4 pound salt pork, cubed

2 cups chopped boiled potatoes

1/2 teaspoon black pepper

Fry salt pork to release all fat. Add potatoes and stir gently. Add pepper.

Sauté 3–5 minutes, stirring gently. Continue cooking, without stirring, until potatoes are browned underneath. Turn potatoes over and sauté the other side until golden brown.

CANDIED CARROTS
SERVES 4–6

6 medium-sized carrots

1/2 cup water

1/2 cup brown sugar

2 tablespoons butter for casserole

Boil carrots in 1/2 cup water for 30 minutes or until fork-tender. Scrape off skins and cut carrots into strips like potatoes for french frying.

Preheat oven to 400° F.

Mix the water and brown sugar in a saucepan and simmer 3 minutes. Place carrots in a buttered 1-quart casserole. Pour the syrup over them.

Bake until candied.

PARSNIPS AND SALT PORK
SERVES 4–6

2 pounds salt pork

6 parsnips

Cut salt pork into small pieces and half-cover with water. Cook until tender. This will take only a few minutes.

Add parsnips cut into 1-inch pieces. Cook approximately 30 minutes or until parsnips are tender.

Serve hot.

FRUITS AND VEGETABLES   61

FRIED EGGPLANT

SERVES 4–6

1 eggplant

Salt

Flour for dredging

2 eggs, beaten

1 teaspoon water

1 cup bread crumbs

Lard for deep frying

Pare eggplant, cut into slices. Sprinkle slices generously with salt. Cover and let stand 1 hour to draw out juices. Drain. Discard juices. Wash eggplant slices with cold water and dry with paper towels. Flour well. Beat the eggs and water together. Dip eggplant slices in the egg mixture, then into the bread crumbs.

Fry in deep lard until browned. Drain on paper towels.

Serve hot.

OKRA AND TOMATOES

SERVES 4–6

2 cups sliced young okra

2 cups skinned, squashed tomatoes

2 tablespoons butter or lard

1 onion, chopped

Salt and pepper to taste

Combine all ingredients in saucepan and simmer over slow heat for 1 hour.

Serve hot.

Chapter 7
SALADS AND
SALAD DRESSINGS

Mother Wit" conjures up a vision of a black wizard in the act of creating savory, appetizing dishes from plain everyday ingredients. Fruits and vegetables were grown on the plantation—how convenient in the planning of a salad! Dressings could be whipped up in moments with eggs, vinegar, and oil.

The following salad is one of Ausiebelle's personal contributions. As she learned it from her mother, I can only assume that this recipe was passed on with ample doses of history and Christian ethics. Ausiebelle lived what she believed and was a strong force in my life.

Whenever she served this salad, she would remind me that what we do in this life matters.

"History skips a lot of chapters, LaMont, but God keeps track of everything."

When I take stock of my personal blessings, this fine, wonderful woman is right at the top of my list.

AUSIEBELLE SALAD

SERVES 4–6

1 cup diced cooked meat

1/2 cup diced cooked potatoes

1/2 cup sliced cooked carrots

1/2 cup cut cooked string beans

1 clove garlic, pressed

1/2 cup french dressing

2 sweet pickles, chopped

1 hard-boiled egg, chopped

1/2 cup mayonnaise, preferably homemade

Pinch of salt, pepper, parsley, grated lemon rind

Lettuce leaves for bedding

Toss the meat and vegetables lightly with the garlic and french dressing. Refrigerate for 1 hour.

Add pickles, egg, mayonnaise, salt, pepper, parsley, and lemon rind.

Serve chilled on a bed of lettuce leaves.

CHICKEN AND FRUIT SALAD

SERVES 4–6

3 cups diced cooked chicken breast

1 orange, peeled and sectioned

1 apple

15 large grapes

15 salted almonds

1 banana

Juice of 1 lemon

1 cup mayonnaise, preferably homemade

Pinch of aniseed

Pinch of parsley

2 tablespoons chopped candied ginger

4–6 lettuce leaves

Put chicken into a large mixing bowl. Remove seeds from orange sections and cut each section in half. Core apple and slice thin. Cut the grapes in half and remove seeds. Split almonds. Slice banana and sprinkle with lemon juice.

Combine fruits and nuts with the chicken. Add the mayonnaise, aniseed, parsley, and candied ginger. Mix gently but thoroughly.

Chill. Put each serving on a lettuce leaf.

CINNAMON APPLE SALAD   SERVES 6

6 firm apples

1 cup water

1 cup cinnamon drops

2 cups sugar

8 tablespoons cream cheese

4 tablespoons mayonnaise, preferably homemade

6 tablespoons chopped pecans

Lettuce beds

6 tablespoons raisins

Core the apples and peel off the skin halfway down. Place in roasting pan on top of the stove. Add the water, cinnamon drops, and sugar.

Cook over low heat 20–30 minutes, turning frequently. When apples are cooked, remove with slotted spoon to refrigerator container and chill.

Soften the cream cheese with the mayonnaise. Add the nuts. Fill the centers of the apples.

Serve each apple on a bed of lettuce. Garnish with the raisins.

GRAPEFRUIT RING SALAD

2½ tablespoons unflavored gelatin

½ cup cold water

1 cup hot water

1½ cups sugar

1½ cups grapefruit juice

½ cup orange juice

¼ cup lemon juice

Pinch of salt

1 cup grapefruit sections

Lettuce leaves

Mayonnaise, preferably homemade

Soak the gelatin in the cold water for 5 minutes. Boil the hot water and sugar for 3 minutes or until clear. Pour over gelatin and stir until dissolved. Cool.

When cool add the grapefruit juice, orange juice, lemon juice, and salt. Drain the grapefruit sections and add to gelatin mixture.

Pour into a salad ring mold and refrigerate.

Decorate a round platter with lettuce leaves. Unmold salad on the lettuce leaves. Serve with mayonnaise in center of ring.

MAYONNAISE

MAKES 1 CUP

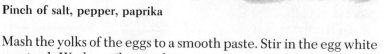

2 hard-boiled egg yolks

1 raw egg white

½ teaspoon dry mustard

½ cup olive oil

½ tablespoon vinegar

Juice of 1 lemon

Pinch of salt, pepper, paprika

Mash the yolks of the eggs to a smooth paste. Stir in the egg white and mustard. Work until smooth.

Beat in the oil by the tablespoon, beating well between each spoonful. When half the oil is used, add the vinegar and lemon juice very slowly, beating constantly. Add the salt, pepper, and paprika. Slowly work in the remaining oil.

Refrigerate until time to serve.

THELMA'S SOUR CREAM DRESSING   MAKES 1 1/4 CUPS

1 cup sour cream

3 tablespoons vinegar

1 1/2 tablespoons sugar

1/2 teaspoon dry mustard

Pinch of salt, pepper, paprika

Slightly whip the sour cream. Mix together the remaining ingredients. Add slowly to the sour cream. Beat until stiff, by hand or machine. Refrigerate.

Chapter 8
BARBECUED MEATS

A barbecue is a festive occasion, a group gathering for food, fellowship, and fun. We tend to think of barbecue as a uniquely American tradition. It's not, nor does barbecue require that meat be cooked over hot coals.

Barbecue dates back centuries to community festivals before towns even existed. Births, deaths, marriages, holidays were all occasions for people to gather and celebrate by roasting an animal over an open fire until it was cooked from the beard *(la barbe)* to the tail *(à queue)*.

French hunters brought this tradition to America, but my great-grandmother Lucinda made it famous. She had an idea to keep the meat moist, tender, and flavorful.

She concocted her own special blend of herbs, spices, and vinegar and combined it with the smoke of different kinds of wood. Instead of just spreading it around, she continued to baste the meat with her own tangy sauce while it cooked. This constant coating of the meat allowed for a crisp outer coating, and also gave it a juicy, tangy, spicy flavor that brought her raves of praise. For thirty years she perfected this sauce and passed it along as her family grew and expanded. Children, grandchildren, great-grandchildren and now great-great-grandchildren all know the secret of this traditional sauce and its special history.

I decided to bottle these unique sauces and marinades to give others the opportunity to enjoy the succulent flavors that have stood the test of time and enhanced family feasts for generations. I have compromised nothing of the excellence of the ingredients or their standards of quality.

The recipes in this chapter are varied and subjective. Any cook on any budget can turn an ordinary meal into a festive repast by correctly following these simple but detailed instructions of barbecuing, using the proper amounts of my spices and sauces. The grade of meat is much less important than the care in preparation.

But let me remind you of the key ingredient handed down by Lucinda herself. The best part of any meal is the tone set by the person who prepares it.

A barbecue is a celebration, a relaxed repast meant to bring people together for good fellowship and good feelings.

That's how it all began, and Lucinda merely followed the tradition when history handed it to her. Ausiebelle and Thelma passed it on to me, and I am passing it on to you. This is my family's legacy of fine food and a history of its meaning.

My sauces, spices, and marinades are available in stores (see the copyright page on how you can get information about them), but they are not necessary for all of the recipes that follow to make your barbecues special occasions. It would please my relative to know that they were used for that reason, just as it pleases me to include you in my family history.

BARBECUED LEG OF LAMB

1 leg of lamb

4 tablespoons vinegar

1/4 teaspoon salt

1/4 teaspoon pepper

2 cups water

1/2 cup flour

1/2 cup catsup

2 tablespoons salt

1 tablespoon Worcestershire sauce

1 large onion, chopped

3 stalks celery, chopped

1/2 teaspoon pepper

Preheat oven to 500° F.

Rub the leg of lamb with vinegar, salt, and pepper. Place the meat on a rack in a shallow roasting pan and roast it at 500° for 30 minutes. Reduce the heat to 350° and continue roasting the lamb, figuring 20 minutes per pound.

Combine the water, flour, catsup, salt, Worcestershire sauce, onions, celery, and pepper. In small batches, purée the mixture in a blender. It will be runny.

When the oven temperature is reduced to 350°, pour the sauce over the lamb. Use it to baste the roast as it cooks. During cooking, the sauce will thicken slightly to a gravy. If desired, after the lamb is cooked drain off the pan juices, spoon the fat from the top, and boil the mixture rapidly to reduce it to the desired consistency.

CHUCK STEAK BARBECUE

SERVES 4–6

2–3 pounds beef chuck steak

1/2 cup red wine

1/2 cup oil

2 tablespoons catsup

2 tablespoons molasses

1 clove garlic, minced

1 teaspoon salt

1/4 teaspoon pepper

Place meat in a shallow baking dish. Combine all other ingredients. Pour over steak. Cover and let marinate for at least 3 hours, turning once.

Remove steak from marinade. Barbecue over medium coals 20 minutes on each side for rare, 25 minutes on each side for medium rare. Brush with remaining marinade during grilling.

Remove meat from grill and carve against grain in thin slices.

BARBECUED LAMB SHANK DINNER

SERVES 4

4 lamb shanks

Flour

Salt, cayenne pepper to taste

3 tablespoons oil

* 2 cups Lucinda's Barbecue Sauce (see page 112)

4 medium potatoes

1 pound fresh green beans

Preheat oven to 350° F.

Dredge the lamb shanks in flour seasoned with salt and cayenne pepper. In a Dutch oven over medium heat, brown the shanks in the oil. Drain off any fat, brush the shanks with the barbecue sauce, and pour a little water into the pan.

Bake the shanks, uncovered, for 1 hour.

Brush the shanks again with barbecue sauce. Peel the potatoes, cut them in quarters, and put them around the shanks. Cover and bake an additional hour.

Brush the shanks with the remaining barbecue sauce. Stem and wash the beans, cut them into bite-size pieces, and place them in the pan with the shanks and potatoes. Uncover and bake 30 minutes more and serve.

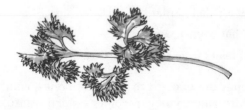

BARBECUED BEEF BRISKET

5 pounds well-trimmed beef brisket

Salt

1/2 cup catsup

1/2 cup finely chopped onions

11/2 teaspoons Liquid Smoke

1/4 teaspoon dried red pepper flakes

1/4 cup brown sugar, packed

11/2 teaspoons salt

1/4 cup vinegar

1 tablespoon Worcestershire sauce

1 bay leaf, crumbled

2 cloves garlic, minced

Rub the brisket all over with salt. Place it on a 20 × 15-inch piece of heavy-duty aluminum foil.

In a bowl stir together the catsup, onions, Liquid Smoke, red pepper flakes, brown sugar, salt, vinegar, Worcestershire, bay leaf, and garlic, blending well.

Pour the mixture over the meat, bring up the sides of the foil, and seal it securely. Place the packet on a barbecue grill over medium-hot coals, 5 inches from the coals. Cook the brisket for about 11/2 hours, turning it once, until the meat is tender. Remove bay leaf before serving.

BARBECUED BEEF BONES   SERVES 2

3/4 cup hot catsup

2 tablespoons Worcestershire sauce

1 tablespoon vinegar

1 1/2 teaspoons celery seed

1 teaspoon Dijon mustard

Dash of hot pepper sauce

4–6 beef bones from cooked rib roast*

In a skillet big enough to hold the bones, combine the catsup, Worcestershire sauce, vinegar, celery seed, mustard, and hot pepper sauce. Over medium heat bring to a boil, then lower heat to simmer.

Add the beef bones and spoon the sauce over them. Cover skillet and simmer the bones for 3 minutes, basting them often with the sauce.

Serve the sauce with the bones. The recipe makes about 1 cup sauce, enough for 4 to 6 bones.

* Uncooked beef bones can be roasted, then simmered in this sauce, which also is delicious on other cuts such as beef short ribs.

EASY BEEF BARBECUE   SERVES 12

1 chuck roast (2 1/2 pounds)

1/2 cup vinegar

1/2 cup sugar

2 medium onions, sliced thin

1/4 cup Worcestershire sauce

1 quart tomatoes, peeled and cut up

or

1 large can (16 ounces) tomatoes with juice

If using a bone-in cut such as 7-bone roast, have the butcher saw the roast into three or four long strips. If using a boneless roast, cut it into three or four large pieces. This will make it easier to shred the meat once it is cooked.

Place the chuck pieces in a heavy Dutch oven. Combine the vinegar, sugar, onions, Worcestershire, and tomatoes and pour them over the meat.

Simmer the mixture over low heat, covered, for at least 4 hours, until the meat is soft and falls from the bones.

Remove the fat and bones and shred the meat with a spoon. Serve the meat on buns. Makes about 12 sandwiches.

OVEN-BARBECUED SHORT RIBS   SERVES 4

3 pounds beef short ribs

1 can (8 ounces) tomato sauce

1$1/2$ teaspoons salt

1 tablespoon prepared mustard

2 tablespoons brown sugar

$1/2$ cup dry red wine

2 tablespoons chopped onions

2 tablespoons vinegar

$1/4$ teaspoon cayenne pepper

Preheat oven to 300° F.

Cut away some of the fat from the ribs. Put the fat in a Dutch oven and render slowly over low heat. Add ribs and brown the ribs in the fat, cooking them slowly and browning them on all sides. Pour off the grease.

Combine the tomato sauce, salt, mustard, brown sugar, wine, onions, vinegar, and cayenne pepper and pour the mixture over the ribs.

Bake the ribs, covered, 2–2$1/2$ hours, or until the meat is very tender.

BARBECUED PORK CHOPS

   8 lean pork chops

   4 tablespoons oil or bacon drippings

   1/2 cup catsup

   1 teaspoon salt

   1 teaspoon celery seed

   1/2 teaspoon nutmeg

   1/3 cup vinegar

   1 cup water

   1 bay leaf

Preheat oven to 325° F.

In a Dutch oven brown the chops over medium heat in oil or bacon drippings. Drain any excess fat from the pan.

Combine the catsup, salt, celery seed, nutmeg, vinegar, water, and bay leaf and pour over the chops. Bake, uncovered, for 1 1/2 hours, turning the chops once. Remove bay leaf before serving.

Chapter 9
BEEF

I have a friend who loves to tease me about my family history. One day she marched in singing, "Oh give me a home, where the buffalo roam, but what would we do without beef?"

In terms of Southern cuisine, she certainly has a point.

My grandmother and mother were keenly aware of the value of a good cow, as almost all parts could be used for a variety of dishes.

The North favored boiling everything. In the South, beef was prepared in a very different manner. Ausiebelle loved to use spicy, tangy sauces to barbecue over an open pit.

All ribs were marinated, smoked, and roasted. Beef was minced into hamburger and made into bulky meat loaf smothered in spicy, creamy sauces. I learned how to make chili, spaghetti, stroganoff, and "stretchers" by watching my mother use eggs, bread crumbs, spices, and milk to make the beef go farther. These meat concoctions were poured over starchy staples like yams, rice, noodles, or potatoes.

Both Ausiebelle and Thelma emphasized that you don't have to have a lot of money to feed large groups of people tasty, nutritious, good food.

Here are some family favorites designed for you to add your own touch to please the palates of your family and friends.

I don't know if the recipes would be the same with buffalo.

LINDA'S DRIED BEEF

SERVES 2–4

1/2 pound dried beef, freshly sliced or packaged

1 tablespoon butter

1 tablespoon flour

1 cup milk

1/2 cup thin cream

Pinch of pepper, dry mustard,
  basil, celery seed

Soak dried beef in boiling water for 5 minutes. Drain and dry on paper towels.

Melt the butter in a saucepan. Stir in the flour and blend well. Gradually add milk and cream, stirring constantly. Cook over low heat until thick. Add pepper, mustard, basil, celery seed, and beef. Cook 10 minutes.

Serve on buttered toast or mashed potatoes.

BROILED HAMBURGER STEAKS

SERVES 4

1 pound ground beef

2 teaspoons chopped onions

Salt and pepper to taste

1/4 teaspoon oregano

1/4 teaspoon garlic powder

1/4 teaspoon parsley

1 tablespoon water

1 tablespoon tomato sauce

1 egg, beaten

4 hamburger rolls

Mix all ingredients together, except the hamburger rolls, and shape into 4 round, flat cakes. Place a piece of butter on top of each cake and broil fast on both sides.

Serve hot on toasted hamburger rolls.

6 eggs

3 pounds ground beef

2 large potatoes, cooked and mashed

Salt and pepper to taste

1/4 teaspoon celery seed

1/4 teaspoon parsley

1/4 teaspoon chives

1 clove garlic, pressed

1 onion, chopped

2 slices bread, diced

1/4 pound sliced bacon

Hard-boil 3 of the eggs. Cool and shell. Mix the remaining 3 eggs together with the ground beef and the other ingredients, except the bacon.

Divide the meat mixture into 2 parts. Flatten each part into a long, narrow rectangle. Lay the whole hard-boiled eggs down the center of 1 rectangle. Cover with the other rectangle and press down.

Preheat oven to 400° F.

Wrap the bacon around the outside of the meat, tying with string. Bake for 1 1/2 hours.

BEEF PICNIC TARTS

Filling

3 1/2 cups ground beef

1 cup cooked, cubed potatoes

1/2 onion, chopped

1/4 cup chopped green pepper

1/4 cup dill pickle relish

1/4 cup catsup

1/4 teaspoon sage

1/2 teaspoon salt

1 teaspoon chili powder

Pastry

1 cup lard

3 cups flour

1/2 cup cold water

1 teaspoon salt

1/2 teaspoon garlic powder

1/2 teaspoon celery seed

Combine meat filling ingredients and mix together.

To make pastry, cut and rub the lard into the flour in a mixing bowl until granular. Add the cold water and seasonings and mix together just enough to include all flour. Handle gently.

Dust a pastry area with enough flour to keep pastry from sticking. Roll out pastry. Cut as many 5–6-inch circles as possible. Re-form leftover pastry and roll out again. Continue until all pastry has been used. Divide circles into 2 piles. Lay 1 stack out on the flat, flour-dusted area.

Preheat oven to 425° F.

Divide meat mixture among half of the pastry circles. Brush edges of pastry with warm water. Lay reserved circles over meat filling. Seal by pressing edges down with a fork. Pierce tops with a fork to allow steam to escape. Place pastries on buttered baking sheets.

Bake for 30 minutes, or until golden brown.

Remove from baking sheets and cool on wire racks. Serve hot or cold, with or without a sauce.

LIVER LAMONT

1 pound calf's liver

Salt and pepper to taste

2 small onions, sliced thin

1 teaspoon chopped parsley

Pinch of allspice, dry mustard, celery seed

Deep fat or oil for frying

Lemon slices

Parsley sprigs

Preheat deep fat to 400° F.

Sprinkle the liver with salt and pepper, onions, parsley, allspice, mustard, and celery seed. Pound seasonings into liver. Let stand for 2 hours, then cut into 1-inch cubes.

Fry in deep fat for about 2 minutes.

Garnish with lemon and parsley.

SWEETBREADS AND MUSHROOMS

SERVES 4–6

1 pair sweetbreads (cubed)

2 tablespoons bacon or chicken fat

2 tablespoons flour

2 cups milk

1 pound fresh mushrooms, sliced

2 tablespoons butter

1/2 cup bread crumbs

4 tablespoons butter

Parboil the sweetbreads 15 minutes. Cool. Remove fat and tissues. Cut into cubes.

Sauté sweetbreads in bacon or chicken fat. Add flour and stir in. Gradually add the milk. Stir constantly until thickened.

Preheat oven to 350° F.

Sauté the mushrooms in the 2 tablespoons of butter. Add to sweetbreads.

Pour into a buttered 1-quart casserole. Cover with bread crumbs. Dot with the 4 tablespoons of butter.

Bake for about 20 minutes or until golden brown.

LEFTOVER BEEF CASSEROLE SERVES 6–8

1 1/2 cups ground beef

1 cup cooked rice

1 1/2 cups skinned, chopped tomatoes

1 large onion, chopped

1/2 green pepper, chopped

2 stalks celery, chopped

Salt and pepper to taste

2 bay leaves

Pinch of horseradish

1 clove garlic, minced

1/4 teaspoon sage

1/2 cup bread crumbs

1/4 cup melted butter

1/2 teaspoon chopped parsley

Preheat oven to 350° F.

Combine all ingredients down to and including sage. Put into 1 1/2-quart buttered casserole.

Combine and mix the bread crumbs, butter, and parsley and use to cover meat mixture. Bake for 1 hour. Remove bay leaves.

Serve hot.

This recipe can also be used for leftover pork, veal, lamb, fish, or chicken.

Chapter 10
PORK

As a little boy, I was intrigued by Ausiebelle's stories of catching pigs for food. What fascinated me was not the gory details of the slaughter, but the inventive ways of preserving the meat for future use.

Ausiebelle knew all about smokehouses and how changing the kind of wood could alter the flavor of the animal. Once the animal was smoked, and thus preserved to last, Ausiebelle would experiment with marinades, spices, and sauces to enhance the flavor.

Her homemade sausage was a wonder to experience, both in the making and the eating. I'd sit and watch her roll and stuff this delicate mixture into delicious strings of good eating.

Even today, pork chops, ribs, roasts, and minced pork dishes remain some of the best-loved meals of the South.

I have included some basic pork recipes as well as casserole-type dishes that I grew up loving. These are things made with beans and apples, scrapple and numerous other ingredients.

Some of my mother's recipes present adventurous eating to the cook seeking inexpensive but tasty, creative dishes. I'll give you fair warning: they are as addictive as chocolate, and will fill your kitchen with the sweet smells of childhood.

ROAST SUCKLING PIG

SERVES 8–10

  1 6-week-old piglet

  Poultry stuffing

  1 red apple

  Candied sweet potatoes

  Apple Ball Sauce

  Sprigs of parsley

Preheat oven to 350° F.

For roast suckling pig, use only the very young pigs not over 6 weeks old.

Scald by immersing in very hot water (not boiling) for 1 minute. Remove from water. Use a very dull knife to scrape off hair. Don't break skin.

Cut a slit from the bottom of the throat to the hind legs. Remove the entrails and other organs. Use care not to break the brains.

Wash thoroughly in cold water. Chill.

Fill with a poultry stuffing of your choice. Sew opening. Put into roasting pan. Roast 30 minutes per pound, basting occasionally.

Remove piglet to a huge serving platter. Polish the apple and place it in the mouth of the piglet. Surround with candied sweet potatoes and Apple Ball Sauce. Decorate the platter with parsley.

APPLE BALL SAUCE

12 ONE-INCH APPLE BALLS

  1 cup sugar

  1 cup water

  Grated rind of 1/2 lemon

  4 cloves

  6 cooking apples to make 11/2 cups 1-inch apple balls

Boil the sugar, water, lemon rind, and cloves together until it makes a soft ball when 1 drop is dropped from the stirring spoon into cold water. This will take approximately 10 minutes.

While syrup is boiling, cut out the apple balls with a 1-inch melon baller. Remove cloves when syrup is ready.

Drop apple balls into syrup and boil until apples are barely cooked, approximately 10 minutes. Avoid overcooking, as the apples will turn to applesauce.

Pour over a pork roast, pork chops, pork casserole or other pork dish.

CHITTERLINGS

SERVES 6–8

Chitterlings are similar to tripe in that they are the small intestines of swine. They are obtainable at most butcher shops during holiday seasons. Chitterlings are a festive dish served for special occasions, especially New Year's, and are said to bring good luck and prosperity for the coming year. We had them every January first when I was growing up. Either Ausiebelle or Thelma would prepare them with the recipe you find right here. The good luck still goes with it.

- 3 pounds chitterlings
- 1 tablespoon whole cloves
- 1 red pepper, chopped
- 2 eggs, beaten
- 1 cup cracker crumbs
- Deep fat for frying

Wash the chitterlings thoroughly. Put into soup kettle. Cover with boiling salted water. Add cloves and red pepper.

Simmer 20 minutes until tender. Drain. Cut chitterlings into pieces the size of oysters. Dip each piece in the beaten eggs, then in cracker crumbs. Set aside for 1/2 hour.

Fry in deep fat until brown.

BROILED HAM

SERVES 4

    1 (1-pound) slice ham

    1 cup milk

    1 cup water

    1/4 teaspoon ground cloves

    1/4 pound salt pork

    2 tablespoons cornstarch

    2 tablespoons cold water

    1/4 cup raisins

Soak ham, trimmed of all fat, in the milk, water, and cloves for 1 hour.

Try out salt pork. Cut into tiny cubes.

Preheat broiler.

Remove ham from liquid and wipe dry. Place on broiler rack and broil slowly. When slightly browned on both sides, remove from rack and put on serving platter.

Heat milk and water ham was soaked in. Combine cornstarch with 2 tablespoons cold water and add, stirring constantly until thickened. Add salt pork and raisins.

BAKED HAM

SERVES 4

    1 (1 1/4-pound) slice of ham, 1 inch thick

    1/2 cup brown sugar

    1 teaspoon dry mustard

    1/4 teaspoon pepper

    1/4 teaspoon curry powder

    2 cups milk

    Parsley sprigs

Preheat oven to 300° F.

Place ham in baking dish. Make a mixture of brown sugar, mustard, pepper, curry powder, and milk. Pour over ham.

Bake for 1 hour. Remove to serving platter and bury in parsley sprigs.

BAKED HAM AND APPLE

SERVES 6

4 large, thin slices ham

1 teaspoon mustard

2 teaspoons vinegar

1/4 teaspoon ginger

1 teaspoon chopped parsley

2 apples, sliced very thin

1/4 cup brown sugar

2 tablespoons butter

1/4 cup honey mixed with 1/4 cup water

Preheat oven to 350° F.

Place ham in baking dish. Mix together the mustard, vinegar, ginger, and parsley. Spread on the ham. Place the apples on the ham. Sprinkle with the brown sugar.

Roll each slice of ham the long way. Fasten with skewers or tie with string. Dot with the butter.

Bake 20–30 minutes. Baste several times with the mixture of honey and water.

Remove to serving platter. Serve hot.

HAM AND PINEAPPLE

SERVES 4

1 slice ham (1 pound or more, 1 inch thick, center cut)

2 cups milk

2 tablespoons butter

1 (no. 21/2) can sliced pineapple

Maraschino cherries or fresh grapes

Soak ham in the milk for 4 hours. Remove the ham from the milk and reserve milk. Melt the butter in a skillet and add ham slice. Sauté until brown on both sides. Transfer ham to serving platter and place in warm oven.

Drain pineapple slices, reserving juice. Put slices in skillet used to cook ham and brown on both sides. Place slices around sides and top of ham.

Mix pineapple juice and the milk with drippings in skillet. Simmer 5 minutes or until well blended. Pour over the ham.

Put a cherry or grape in the hole of each pineapple ring and around the base of serving platter.

LUCINDA'S HAM SHOULDER

SERVES 8–10

1 ham shoulder (10–12 pounds)

1/4 cup vinegar

Whole cloves

1/4 cup fine cracker crumbs

1/4 cup brown sugar

Sprinkle of pepper

1/4 cup sherry

Soak the ham shoulder with the vinegar for 12 hours in water to cover.

Bring to a fast boil. Turn to low heat and simmer 4–5 hours or until tender. Cool in its own juice.

Preheat oven to 450° F.

Place ham shoulder in roasting pan. Remove skin and make crisscross gashes in the fat on top and sides of ham with a sharp knife. Stick whole cloves between the gashes.

Combine the cracker crumbs, brown sugar, and pepper. Sprinkle on top of ham. Sprinkle with sherry.

Bake for 20 minutes, or until bubbly and syrupy.

BREADED PORK

1 pound pork, raw or cooked

1 clove garlic, pressed

1 tablespoon prepared mustard

2 cups bread crumbs

3 tablespoons cooking oil

3 tablespoons vinegar or lemon juice

4 tablespoons flour

1/4 teaspoon sage

1 egg, beaten

1/4 cup milk

1 tablespoon peanut oil or chicken fat

Deep fat for frying

Cut pork into thin slices. Spread both sides with garlic and mustard. Pat both sides with 1 cup of the bread crumbs.

Sauté in the cooking oil until brown. Remove from pan and place on flat surface. Sprinkle with vinegar or lemon juice. Let stand 15 minutes.

Dredge meat in mixture of flour and sage. Dip in mixture of the egg, milk, and peanut oil. Roll in remaining cup of bread crumbs. Deep-fry until golden brown. Drain on paper towels. Serve hot.

LUCINDA'S SCRAPPLE

3 pounds pork bone(s) with small amount
   of meat and fat clinging to bone

Water to cover

1 teaspoon salt

1/2 teaspoon pepper

1 onion, chopped

1 teaspoon sugar

2 cups yellow cornmeal

Pork fat for frying

Simmer the pork bone or bones in water to cover, until some of the meat drops from the bones. Pick remaining meat and fat from bones and set aside.

Measure broth. If more than 4 cups, boil down to 4 cups. If less, add enough water to make 4 cups. Add to the liquid the salt, pepper, onions, and sugar. Add the cornmeal, stirring constantly. Mixture will thicken almost immediately.

Chop the meat and fat and add to cornmeal mixture. Mix thoroughly. This is now scrapple.

Pour the hot scrapple into dampened oblong baking pan. Let stand until cool. Refrigerate.

Unmold on floured surface. Slice into 1/4-inch slices. Flour each slice and brown in hot pork fat. Serve immediately.

Chapter 11
VEAL

My mother used to say that veal was the most tender meat to eat and the sweetest one to season. I can remember wondering what that meant as she would pound away at a cutlet or use a thick knife on a chop. But eating one of her specially prepared veal dishes caused everything she said to fall into place.

Veal is a sweet, tender meat which requires special preparation to bring out the subtleties of its flavor. I have included a recipe called Veal Chops in Buttered Paper which my mother would cook for large groups of people in Chicago when I was a boy. They would rave over this dish, just as I would relish eating it in the kitchen.

I have also included recipes for different uses of veal—fricassee, stuffed chops, and leg of veal.

Veal is a special kind of meat that takes careful preparation to be truly appreciated. I like to work with veal, perhaps because it reminds me of my mother's strength which would inevitably produce something delicious.

LINDA'S VEAL FRICASSEE

Veal is baby cow, therefore the meat is ever so much more tender than the adult. It is also lighter in color, of a blander flavor, and rarely needs to be tenderized.

2 pounds veal loin

3 cups water

1 onion, chopped

2 stalks celery, chopped

2 carrots, chopped

Pinch of salt and pepper

Grated rind of 1 lemon

Flour for dredging

3 tablespoons butter or bacon fat

Brown Sauce

Put veal into soup kettle. Add water, onions, celery, and carrots. Simmer 1 hour.

Strain broth and reserve broth and vegetables for the Brown Sauce.

Rub the salt, pepper, and lemon rind into the meat. Cut meat into bite-size pieces and dredge with flour. Sauté in the butter or bacon fat until delicate brown. Put into serving dish.

Serve with Brown Sauce.

Brown Sauce:

2 cups veal broth

2 tablespoons flour

2 tablespoons butter

Vegetables from veal broth

Salt and pepper to taste

Heat veal broth in saucepan. In another saucepan brown the flour in butter. Add veal broth slowly, stirring constantly until smooth.

Put vegetables through blender or sieve. Add to brown sauce. Salt and pepper to taste.

Put into gravy bowl and serve with the veal.

DIXIE VEAL, HAM, AND CHEESE ROLLS

3 pounds veal round steak, 1/4 inch thick

2 cloves garlic, pressed

12 pieces ham, sliced thin

12 pieces cheese, sliced thin

Flour for dredging

2 eggs, beaten

3 tablespoons milk

1/2 teaspoon horseradish

1 cup bread crumbs

1/4 teaspoon poultry seasoning

1 can condensed cream of mushroom soup

2 tablespoons white wine

1/2 cup milk

Sprinkle of paprika

Preheat oven to 350° F.

Pound veal with garlic into 1/8-inch thickness. Cut into 12 even pieces. Top each piece of veal with thin slice of ham. Top each with thin slice of cheese. Roll up veal pieces with ham and cheese inside. Secure with toothpicks, tie with thread. Dredge each roll with flour.

Combine the eggs, milk, and horseradish together. Roll each meat roll in this egg wash.

Mix bread crumbs and poultry seasoning together. Roll each meat roll in the bread crumbs. Place seam side down in baking dish.

Combine and bring to boil the mushroom soup, white wine, and milk. Pour around meat rolls. Cover baking dish.

Bake for 1 hour. Uncover and sprinkle with paprika. Bake another 10 minutes or until crumbs are a golden brown.

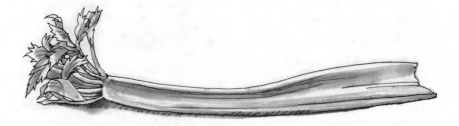

VEAL CHOPS IN BUTTERED PAPER   SERVES 25

25 thin veal chops

2 tablespoons chopped parsley

2 tablespoons chopped onions

2 tablespoons chopped chives

3/4 cup chopped mushrooms

1/2 teaspoon salt

1/4 teaspoon pepper

1/2 teaspoon ground ginger

Butter for spreading

25 slices of bread

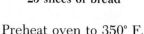

Preheat oven to 350° F.

Dredge each chop in mixture of the parsley, onions, chives, mushrooms, salt, pepper, and ginger.

Lay out 25 sheets of parchment paper, big enough to wrap each chop and to tuck under. Spread butter on each paper. Place a buttered slice of bread on each paper. Place a chop on each slice of bread. Fold papers over and around chops so that no steam or juice can escape.

Bake for 1 1/2 hours. Serve the chops wrapped in the parchment paper.

LOUISIANA VEAL CHOPS   SERVES 12

1/2 cup peanut oil

2 cloves garlic, crushed

1/2 teaspoon salt

1/4 teaspoon pepper

1/4 teaspoon oregano

12 veal loin chops

Flour for dredging

Peanut oil for sautéing

1 cup chicken broth

1/4 cup cornstarch

Combine and mix the peanut oil, garlic, salt, pepper, and oregano. Refrigerate 2–3 hours or overnight.

Dredge the chops in flour. Brown them in the peanut oil. Pour marinade over meat. Cover. Simmer 30 minutes.

Blend the chicken broth and cornstarch and stir into the marinade. Bring to a boil, stirring constantly, to thicken.

Serve hot.

STUFFED VEAL CHOPS SERVES 6

6 veal chops, very thick

1/4 cup bread crumbs

1/4 cup chopped pecans

1/4 teaspoon salt

1/4 teaspoon ground ginger

1/2 cup apple juice

1/4 cup chopped onion

1 clove garlic, pressed

Flour for dredging

2 tablespoons peanut oil

Parsley sprigs

Pimento, chopped

Slit chops with a sharp knife to make horizontal pockets.

Mix together the bread crumbs, pecans, salt, ginger, apple juice, onion, and garlic. Stuff into veal pockets. Dredge chops with the flour.

Sauté in the peanut oil. Cover the pan and simmer 45 minutes. Remove to serving platter.

Garnish with the parsley sprigs and chopped pimento.

LEG OF VEAL ROAST

4-pound leg of veal

1 clove garlic, minced

1/4 cup vinegar

1/2 teaspoon salt

1/4 teaspoon pepper

1 teaspoon paprika

1/4 pound suet, ground

14 ounces mushrooms, sliced

1/2 cup sliced onions

1/2 cup chopped celery

1/4 cup chopped green tomatoes

6 tablespoons butter

1/2 teaspoon grated lemon rind

Parsley sprigs

Preheat oven to 325° F.

Put veal on open rack in roasting pan. Rub with the garlic and mixture of vinegar, salt, pepper, paprika, and suet.

Bake for 2 hours and 20 minutes.

Sauté the mushrooms, onions, celery, green tomatoes in the butter. Add lemon rind.

Put meat on serving platter. Cover with the mushroom mixture. Decorate with the parsley sprigs.

EARTHY VEAL CUTLETS

12 veal cutlets, boned

1 clove garlic, minced

1 cup potato flakes

1/2 teaspoon paprika

1/2 teaspoon ground ginger

1/2 teaspoon salt

1/2 cup butter

1 pound mushrooms, sliced

Juice of 2 lemons

1 cup chicken broth

Grated rind of 1 lemon

Preheat oven to 350° F.

Pound cutlets until thin. Dredge in mixture of garlic, potato flakes, paprika, ginger, and salt.

Sauté in the butter and lay in large baking pan. Sprinkle with the mushrooms and a mixture of lemon juice and chicken broth. Cover.

Bake for 1 hour or until meat is tender. Put on large serving platter. Garnish with lemon rind.

GRANDMOTHER'S VEAL

SERVES 25

6 1/4 pounds veal, cut into 1-inch cubes

1/2 cup butter

1/4 cup paprika

1 teaspoon salt

1 teaspoon pepper

1 teaspoon horseradish

2 cloves garlic, minced

6 (10 1/2-ounce) cans condensed cream of mushroom soup

6 cups sliced onions

1/2 cup sherry

2 cups sour cream

1/4 teaspoon pepper

4 cups (1 quart) cooked rice

Chives for garnishing

Preheat oven to 350° F.

Sauté veal in butter in roasting pan. Add the paprika, salt, pepper, horseradish, and garlic. Mix the mushroom soup and onions and spread over meat.

Bake for 45 minutes, covered. Pour sherry over meat and bake another 35 minutes, uncovered.

Mix sour cream and pepper and pour over meat. Bake another 10 minutes.

Serve on hot boiled rice. Garnish with chopped chives.

Chapter 12
MEAT SAUCES

Any meat dish can be enhanced by a sauce.

There are so many varieties of tastes, from the zesty and piquant to the creamy and the subtle.

Here are some family favorites designed to please a host of palates. Most of these recipes have been handed down from generation to generation. We have always enjoyed them, and sincerely wish that you will too.

LUCINDA'S BARBECUE SAUCE

1/4 pound (1 stick) butter

1 cup vinegar

1 sour pickle, finely chopped

2 tablespoons chopped onion

2 tablespoons hot pepper sauce

2 tablespoons chili sauce

4 slices lemon

1 teaspoon brown sugar

1 green pepper, finely chopped

1/4 teaspoon salt

1/4 teaspoon pepper

1/4 teaspoon cumin seeds

1 teaspoon paprika

1 teaspoon parsley

1/2 teaspoon ginger

1 clove garlic, chopped

Combine all ingredients in a saucepan and mix thoroughly. Stir constantly over low heat and simmer until butter melts.

Place in the top of a double boiler to keep warm until ready to use.

HORSERADISH SAUCE

MAKES 1 1/2 CUPS

2 tablespoons finely chopped onion

3 tablespoons butter

1 cup cream or soup stock

2 egg yolks, well beaten

1/2 cup grated fresh horseradish

Sauté onion in butter until translucent. Add cream or soup stock and simmer 5 minutes.

Strain through a fine sieve. Pour onto egg yolks, stirring until well blended.

Cook over low heat until thick, stirring constantly. Add the horseradish. Cook just long enough to blend well.

Serve with beef, other meats, and fish.

LINDA'S HOLLANDAISE SAUCE   MAKES 1 CUP

4 egg yolks

1/2 cup butter, melted

1/4 teaspoon salt

Dash of black pepper

2 tablespoons lemon juice

In top of double boiler, beat the egg yolks. Slowly add the melted butter. Stir in the salt and pepper. Cook over low heat, stirring constantly, until sauce thickens. Remove from heat and stir in lemon juice.

Serve on vegetables and casseroles.

This is a sauce which must be served as soon as finished. Should the sauce separate, it may be brought together again if a small amount of hot, thin cream is added and beaten well.

WHITE SAUCE   MAKES 1 1/2 CUPS

1 1/2 cups milk

2 tablespoons butter

2 tablespoons flour

1/2 teaspoon salt

1/4 teaspoon pepper

Scald the milk in a saucepan over low heat.

Melt the butter in another saucepan. Add the flour to the butter and mix until well blended. Add salt and pepper.

Add the milk slowly to the flour and butter mixture, stirring constantly. When thickened, remove from heat and beat until creamy and all lumps have disappeared.

MUSHROOM SAUCE

MAKES 1¹/2 CUPS

1¹/2 cups sliced fresh mushrooms

4 tablespoons butter

3 tablespoons flour

1 cup thin cream or milk

Pinch of salt and pepper

Sauté mushrooms in butter.

Slightly brown the flour in saucepan and add slowly to mushrooms, stirring constantly.

Add the thin cream and cook until thickened. Season to taste with salt and pepper.

This is a basic sauce that can be used for most meats.

TOMATO SAUCE

MAKES 2 CUPS

3 tablespoons fat (butter, bacon fat,
    chicken fat, salt pork, or lard)

3 tablespoons flour

2 cups crushed, peeled tomatoes

1 tablespoon brown sugar

1/4 teaspoon ground cloves

1/2 teaspoon allspice

Salt and pepper to taste

Melt the fat in saucepan. Add the flour, mixing until well blended. Add the tomatoes and remaining ingredients. Stir vigorously.

Simmer 5 minutes, stirring frequently.

This sauce is good with any pasta dish, and with dishes where a tomato taste will improve the flavor.

RAISIN SAUCE FOR HAM

MAKES 2 CUPS

1 cup raisins

1 cup water

5 cloves

3/4 cup brown sugar

1 teaspoon cornstarch

1/4 teaspoon salt

1 tablespoon butter

1 tablespoon vinegar

1/4 teaspoon chili powder

Cover the raisins with the water, add cloves and simmer for 10 minutes.

Mix together the brown sugar, cornstarch, and salt. Add to raisins and water and stir until slightly thickened. Add remaining ingredients and bring to a boil.

FROZEN MINT ICE FOR LAMB

MAKES 41/2 CUPS

5 sprays fresh mint

1/2 cup lemon juice

1/2 cup confectioner's sugar

4 cups water

A dash of green vegetable coloring (optional)

1/4 teaspoon peppermint extract

Pinch of salt

Wash and pick the mint leaves from the stems. Soak the leaves in the lemon juice for 1/2 hour. Strain, pressing leaves to conserve all juice. Discard the leaves.

Dissolve the sugar in the water and add to the strained lemon juice.

Just before freezing, add the food coloring, peppermint extract, and salt. Pour into tiny water containers and freeze for 12 hours.

Chapter 13
CHICKEN

It is true that there is nothing more delicious than real Southern-fried chicken like Ausiebelle used to make from the leftover batter of the morning's pancakes. Naturally, I have included this recipe along with a host of others.

When my great-grandmother lived and worked on a plantation, chickens roamed around everywhere, feeding on corn kernels and grains. They were a practical staple because they required so little care, laid eggs, and could be transformed into any number of dishes.

Ausiebelle would relate with great pride that any black woman who worked in the kitchen could wring a chicken's neck and have it plucked and in the pot in no time.

Today we have it a little easier, but the variety of serving styles remains impressive.

I've included real Southern delights, from Fried Chicken Maryland to Miss Ausiebelle's Chicken Pot Casserole. There is something for every palate here.

MISS AUSIEBELLE'S CHICKEN POT CASSEROLE

SERVES 6–8

2¹/₂ tablespoons instant tapioca

¹/₄ teaspoon salt

Dash of pepper and paprika

2 cups cooked chicken, cut in pieces

1¹/₄ cups milk or chicken stock

2 tablespoons melted butter

¹/₄ teaspoon sugar

6 unbaked baking powder biscuits, rolled ¹/₄ inch thick

Preheat oven to 425° F.

Combine all the ingredients except the biscuits, in the order given. Turn into a 1-quart buttered casserole.

Bake for 10 minutes, stirring mixture twice. Place biscuits on top of chicken. Bake for another 20 minutes, or until biscuits are golden brown.

FRIED CHICKEN MARYLAND

SERVES 4–6

1 (2-pound) chicken

Salt and pepper

Flour for dredging

3 tablespoons cooking oil

1 cup boiling water

1 teaspoon parsley

¹/₄ teaspoon sage

Pinch of cumin seeds and ground cloves

Cut chicken into quarters. Wash parts and dry with paper towels. Sprinkle with salt and pepper, and dredge in flour.

In Dutch oven, sauté chicken on all sides in cooking oil. Add the water, parsley, sage, cumin seeds, and cloves.

Simmer for 1 hour. Remove lid and simmer until quite dry.

CHILIED CHICKEN

SERVES 8–10

1 (2-pound) chicken

Water to cover

2 cups peeled, crushed tomatoes

1/2 teaspoon salt

3 cloves garlic, chopped

3 large onions, chopped

4 teaspoons chili powder

4 cups (1 quart) red kidney beans, cooked or canned

Crackers

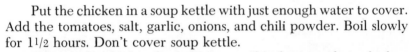

Put the chicken in a soup kettle with just enough water to cover. Add the tomatoes, salt, garlic, onions, and chili powder. Boil slowly for 1 1/2 hours. Don't cover soup kettle.

Remove the chicken from the water. Skin, bone, and cut chicken into bite-size pieces. Return chicken to water. Simmer, uncovered, for 1/2 hour, stirring frequently.

Add kidney beans. Simmer another 10 minutes.

Serve in bowls with crackers.

LUCINDA'S CHICKEN CASSEROLE

SERVES 3–4

2 tablespoons butter

1 1/2 tablespoons flour

1 cup chicken stock, heated

1/4 teaspoon ground cloves

2 cups chopped cooked chicken

Buttered toast

Preheat oven to 350° F.

Melt the butter in a saucepan. Add the flour and stir to blend. Add stock and cloves. Stir thoroughly to make the sauce smooth and well blended. When thick add the chicken. Too much stirring will separate the chicken pieces.

Pour into a buttered, 1-quart casserole. Bake until golden brown. Serve in casserole, garnished with slices of buttered toast.

CHICKEN TERRAPIN

2 pairs sweetbreads

1/2 teaspoon salt

1/4 teaspoon pepper

Pinch of cloves and grated orange rind

1 large chicken

1 quart cream

1 tablespoon cornstarch mixed with 1 tablespoon cold water

2 egg yolks, beaten

1 tablespoon melted butter

1 wineglass sherry

Preheat oven to 350° F.

Parboil the sweetbreads. Cool. Remove the membrane. Cut sweetbreads into small pieces. Sprinkle with the salt, pepper, cloves, and orange rind.

Boil the chicken for 1 hour. Cool. Skin chicken, remove meat from bones, and cut into small pieces. Add to the sweetbreads. Pour into casserole and keep hot in oven.

Place cream in top of double boiler over low heat. Thicken with the cornstarch, stirring constantly. Add the egg yolks and butter. When well thickened, mix into the chicken and sweetbreads. Reheat in oven for about 1/2 hour.

Just before serving, add the wine and stir gently until well blended.

This dish can be served either on toast or in patty shells.

Chapter 14
GAME

When I was little, Ausiebelle used to tell me stories of hunting wild game in the South. I was fascinated by the idea of deer, wild ducks and geese, partridges, doves, and wild turkey. She swore that these were better than any poultry and that the most elegant dinners came from trapping these animals.

It wasn't until I was older that I fully came to appreciate boar and pheasant as some of the finest delicacies served in elegant homes and restaurants.

What distinguishes these dishes from most staples is the creative combining of herbs and spices in them, plus the distinctive flavors of the smoke of different firewoods.

Ausiebelle used to say these were fancy dishes enhanced with nuances of tastes and textures. These were the dishes for dinner parties, celebrations, or special occasions.

I invite you to partake of some family favorites.

AUSIEBELLE'S BELGIAN HARE

1 rabbit

Salt and pepper

Flour for dredging

1 egg, beaten

Cracker crumbs

3 tablespoons lard

1 onion, chopped

1 bay leaf

1/4 teaspoon ground cloves

1 clove garlic, minced

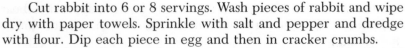

Preheat oven to 350° F.

Cut rabbit into 6 or 8 servings. Wash pieces of rabbit and wipe dry with paper towels. Sprinkle with salt and pepper and dredge with flour. Dip each piece in egg and then in cracker crumbs.

Heat the lard in Dutch oven. Sauté the onions in the lard. Add bay leaf, cloves, and garlic.

Add the meat and roast for 2 hours, turning once. Remove the bay leaf. Serve hot.

OPOSSUM

Imagine laying a trap for an opossum? Yet that particular animal wasn't a stranger to the Southern table. Ducks went quacking around the yard gobbling up the snails and spiders, and were easy victims for the roasting pan. Partridge, pigeon, and squab were abundant and were easily raised or hunted. All kinds of game were prolific. Roasted in herbs and spices, they were delicious and could be served many times without tiring those who partook of them. And their stuffings are as individual as the birds.

Wild game has always been a Southern delicacy, and opossum is one of its special treats, even today. Both Ausiebelle and Thelma grew up with the wonders of opossum stew in their repertoire of wild game recipes. One look at a map of the South shows you how easily wild game could be procured for festive eating. Hunting and trapping have always been popular activities.

Today it is usually necessary to rely on specialty shops in large cities to obtain an exotic meat like opossum, but it can be done. Opossum tastes a lot like pork, but spicier. Here is a recipe for the adventuresome eater in search of a succulent culinary experience with deep roots in history.

1 opossum

Opossum liver

Bread Stuffing (see page 135)

Bacon fat

Salt and pepper

4 slices of bacon

Strong thread for trussing

Preheat oven to 350° F.

Skin opossum and slit open from throat down through the stomach to the hind legs. Remove innards and discard all but liver. Wash thoroughly. Dry with paper towels. Boil liver 5–10 minutes, then chop and add to Bread Stuffing.

Rub opossum inside and out with the bacon fat, salt, and pepper.

Put into roasting pan. Fill opossum with Bread Stuffing. Sew up the opossum with thread or use skewers. Lace with bacon. Add 1 quart of hot water to pan.

Roast 1 1/2 hours or until tender. Baste every 15 minutes. Put on serving platter. Serve hot.

LAMONT'S ROAST DUCK   SERVES 4

1 large duck

Salt and pepper

1 tablespoon paprika

2 tablespoons ground ginger

1 whole onion, peeled

10 cloves

1 cooking apple, cored and quartered

1 orange, quartered, skin and all

1 clove garlic

2 cups water

1 lemon, sliced

2 tablespoons flour mixed with 2 tablespoons water

1/4 teaspoon allspice

Preheat oven to 350° F.

Clean duck as you would any fowl. Rub inside and out with salt, pepper, paprika, and ginger.

Peel onion and stick with the cloves. Place in cavity. Place apple, orange, and garlic clove in cavity. Place duck in roaster with 1 cup of water and the lemon slices.

Roast duck 20 minutes to the pound. Remove duck from roaster to serving platter.

Pour off fat. Add the other cup of water to roaster. Heat slowly, scraping bottom and sides of pan to use all the drippings.

Mix the flour, water, and allspice. Stir into hot water and beat to avoid lumps. Pour over the duck or put into gravy bowl.

Serve hot.

ROAST PARTRIDGE   SERVES 4

4 partridges

Salt and pepper

2 tablespoons horseradish

4 strips bacon

1 cup water

1 cup sour cream

Orange marmalade

Preheat oven to 350° F.

Wash insides of partridges. Dry with paper towels. Rub inside and out with salt, pepper, and horseradish. Pin a strip of bacon over the breast of each partridge. Put into roasting pan with the water.

Roast 40 minutes, basting every 5 minutes.

When birds and gravy are a rich brown, pour cream over them. Let cream bubble up for 3 minutes. Baste birds once more.

Serve the partridge on toast with cream gravy.

Serve with orange marmalade on the side.

PIGEON PIE

4 squab

4 cups boiling water

4 tablespoons butter

Rich Pastry Dough

2 tablespoons melted butter

2 tablespoons flour

1 cup milk, heated

Salt and pepper

8 tiny onions, peeled

1/4 cup chopped pimento

1/2 cup grated sharp cheese

Preheat oven to 400° F.

Dress squab. Wash inside and out. Put into a large roasting pan with 4 cups boiling water. Simmer, covered, 45 minutes, or until fork-tender. Remove from water and drain.

Sauté boiled squab in butter until brown and crispy.

Line a 9-inch pie pan with half of the Rich Pastry Dough. Arrange the fried squab in the pie plate.

Blend the melted butter and flour together. Blend in the heated milk, salt, and pepper. Heat and blend together, stirring vigorously to eliminate lumps. Pour mixture over squab. Arrange onions and pimento around squab.

Bake 45 minutes, then remove from oven and sprinkle with cheese. Lower oven to 350° F. Return to oven and bake until cheese begins to bubble and turn golden brown.

Rich Pastry Dough

3 cups flour

1/2 cup butter

1/2 teaspoon salt

1/2 cup milk

Blend flour, butter, and salt. Add the milk and blend gently only until the flour is absorbed. Roll out to fit a 9-inch pie plate.

ROAST SQUAB WITH RICE

SERVES 4

4 squab

6 slices bacon, cut

1 onion, chopped

3/4 cup chopped celery

2 cups rice

4 cups chicken stock

4 eggs

Salt and pepper to taste

Mustard pickle juice

Preheat oven to 350° F.

Dress the squab, cleaning them thoroughly. Fry bacon until crisp. Remove bacon and sauté the onion and celery.

Boil the rice in the chicken stock 20 minutes. Add the bacon, onion, and celery.

Beat the eggs and add them to the rice. Season with salt and pepper.

Stuff the squab with the rice mixture and make mounds, in the roasting pan, of the remaining filling on which to lay the squab.

Bake for about 25 minutes, basting the squab frequently with mustard pickle juice.

Chapter 15
BREADS
AND STUFFINGS

I was raised in a Christian family where our daily bread was something we prepared ourselves and gave thanks for later.

Both my mother and Ausiebelle introduced me to the joys of kneading bread as a little boy, the pleasures of smelling it in the oven and the sheer delight in the act of baking bread. I still like the serenity of working with dough and the satisfaction of serving hot baked bread to loved ones and friends.

My mother taught me something I didn't know. Black slave women introduced the use of corn in baking bread. Even to this day, many countries consider corn only suitable for animal consumption. We have a legacy of corn breads, skillet corn breads, hoecakes, corn pones, dodgers, cracklin' corn muffins, cakes, and spoon breads.

This chapter includes a variety of breads that are easy to prepare. They are a delight to serve because of the vast differences in tastes, smell, and textures. Many creative combinations of grains and shortenings were used in the loving and careful preparations of these breads.

S tuffing game or poultry served a dual role in Southern cooking. By filling the meat with crushed bread, herbs, and spices, all the succulent juices were preserved as it baked in the oven. Stuffing also extended the meat to feed more people for the same amount of money.

Good stuffing has taken on a glamour of its own. Here is where a cook can add her own touch—a bit of this, a bit of that combined to make a special stuffing for any type of meat. Thelma and Ausiebelle both prided themselves on their stuffings. Some of their favorites have been included here. People used to comment that their original stuffings were the best part of the meal.

They are certainly one of the tastiest.

CRACKLIN' BREAD

SERVES 6–8

1 1/2 cups white cornmeal

3/4 cup wheat flour

1/2 teaspoon baking soda

1/4 teaspoon salt

1 cup sour milk

1 cup cracklings, chopped*

Clover or orange honey

Preheat oven to 400° F.

Mix and sift together the dry ingredients. Add the milk and stir well. Stir in the cracklings.

Butter a 1-quart casserole and fill with crackling mixture.

Bake 30 minutes. Serve hot with clover or orange honey.

* Cracklings are the crunchy pieces of pork and fat remaining after the lard has been rendered from the pork.

SOUTHERN SPOON BREAD

SERVES 6–8

2 cups white cornmeal

2 cups boiling water

3 tablespoons butter

1/2 teaspoon salt

1 1/2 cups milk

3 eggs, separated

Butter to grease casserole

Preheat oven to 350° F.

Sift the meal 3 times and add slowly to the boiling water. Stir constantly so it won't lump. Add the butter and salt. Mix until smooth. Slowly add and mix in the milk. Beat mixture until light. Beat the egg yolks and stir into the batter. Whip the egg whites until soft peaks form, then fold into batter.

Pour into buttered 2-quart casserole. Bake for 30 minutes or until light brown. Serve hot or cold.

SHORTNIN' BREAD

   1/2 cup brown sugar

   1 cup (2 sticks) butter, melted

   2 cups flour

Preheat oven to 325°.

   Combine sugar and butter and add flour, mixing well. Place on floured surface and pat into 1/2-inch thickness. Cut into desired shapes.

   Bake 20–25 minutes or until light brown.

BREAD STUFFING

   4 cups (1 quart) stale bread

   1/2 teaspoon salt

   1/4 teaspoon pepper

   3 tablespoons poultry seasoning

   1 teaspoon chopped parsley

   1 onion, chopped

   2 stalks celery, chopped

   1 clove garlic, minced

   1/4 cup melted butter

   1 egg, beaten

   Soak bread in water to cover about 1/2 hour. Squeeze dry.

   Combine all ingredients in large mixing bowl. Use as gentle a hand as possible.

Half bread crumbs and half cracker crumbs can be used. Bacon fat instead of butter is sometimes used.

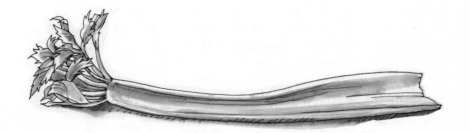

POTATO STUFFING

MAKES 4 CUPS

5 potatoes, cooked, peeled, and mashed

1 egg, beaten

2 teaspoons parsley

Pinch of tarragon

1/2 onion, chopped

1/4 cup chopped celery

1/4 cup chopped green pepper

2 tablespoons butter

1 cup cracker crumbs

Salt and pepper to taste

Mix the potatoes, egg, parsley, and tarragon in mixing bowl.

Sauté the onions, celery, and green peppers in the butter. Add the cracker crumbs and brown. Mix in the salt and pepper. Add to the potato mixture.

Sauté the whole mixture for 5 minutes.

Use this for stuffing game and fowl.

OYSTER STUFFING

MAKES 5 1/2 CUPS

3/4 cup melted butter

2 cups oysters

2 tablespoons chopped onion

3 tablespoons chopped parsley

1 1/2 cups chopped celery

6 cups stale bread crumbs

Salt and pepper to taste

Melt the butter and sauté the oysters until edges curl, being careful not to overcook. Remove oysters from sauté pan. Chop on breadboard and put into mixing bowl.

Sauté onions, parsley, and celery until onions are translucent. Add the bread crumbs, stirring well. Heat. Add salt and pepper.

Use for stuffing fowl or game.

CHESTNUT STUFFING

MAKES ENOUGH FOR
10-POUND TURKEY

1 pound chestnuts

1/4 cup cooking oil

1/4 cup butter

2 cups chopped celery

1/2 cup chopped onions

1 teaspoon chopped parsley

1 egg, beaten

6 cups bread crumbs

Salt and pepper to taste

Crack the chestnut shells with a hammer. Boil chestnuts for 20 minutes. Remove shells. Sauté skins on chestnuts in oil while the nuts are still hot. Remove the skins from the nuts and discard. Chop the chestnuts.

In the same skillet, melt the butter and sauté together the celery, onions, parsley, egg, bread crumbs, and chestnuts. Season with the salt and pepper. Stir mixture over a low heat until thoroughly mixed and heated. Let cool, then stuff chicken, turkey, or game.

Chapter 16
FISH AND SHELLFISH

If I heard it once, I heard it a hundred times from both my grandmother and my mother:

The secret of any good seafood dish is the freshness of the fish. No sauces or spices will make up for lack of freshness.

Ausiebelle was raised in the South around the many rivers and bays, wherever the land touched the seas. Shellfish were in abundance; oysters, crabs, shrimp, and crayfish were easily available. From the rivers, catfish, fat perch, bream and black bass were in plentiful supply.

The variety of serving styles is astounding. Within these pages you will find recipes that transform fresh fish into succulent seafood dishes that are true culinary wonders.

Let me repeat for Ausiebelle, "Make sure the seafood is fresh."

THELMA'S DEVILED CRAB   SERVES 4

1 tablespoon melted butter

1 tablespoon flour

1/2 cup light cream, warmed

1/2 teaspoon mustard

1/4 teaspoon celery seed

Salt and pepper to taste

2 cups (1 pint) crabmeat, cooked and picked over

2 hard-boiled eggs, peeled and chopped

1/2 teaspoon chopped parsley

Dash of hot pepper sauce

1/2 cup cracker crumbs

1/2 cup melted butter

Preheat oven to 350° F.

Mix butter and flour in saucepan over low heat. Add light cream, stirring constantly until thickened. Add mustard, celery seed, salt, and pepper. Add crabmeat, eggs, parsley, and hot pepper sauce. Stir until well mixed.

Divide among 4 tiny individual baking dishes. Sprinkle with the cracker crumbs. Cover with the butter. Bake 15 minutes until well browned. Serve hot.

SHRIMP MOLD   SERVES 8–10

4 cups cooked shrimp, shelled and deveined

Salt and pepper to taste

Pinch of mace

3 tablespoons melted butter

Mash shrimp with a fork. Put into saucepan. Add salt, pepper, and mace. Heat thoroughly, stirring gently.

Fill buttered bread pan with shrimp mixture and press down firmly with back of a spoon. Pour butter over top. Refrigerate until cold and firm.

Unmold and slice.

Served on cocktail crackers, this mixture makes fantastic hors d'oeuvres.

SHRIMP AND RICE CROQUETTES   SERVES 4

1 cup rice

1 tablespoon butter

2 cups cooked shrimp, shelled and deveined

2 eggs, beaten separately

Salt and pepper to taste

1/4 teaspoon nutmeg

1 rose geranium leaf, chopped

Flour for dredging

Cracker crumbs for dredging

Deep fat for frying

Cook rice according to manufacturer's directions. Add butter while hot.

Chop the shrimp fine. Add one of the beaten eggs, salt, pepper, nutmeg, and chopped geranium leaf. Mix thoroughly with the rice.

Roll into croquettes the size of a walnut. Roll first in the flour, then in the other egg, then in cracker crumbs. Refrigerate 3–4 hours.

Fry in deep fat until golden brown. Drain on paper towels.

LAMONT'S OYSTER LOAF

SERVES 4–6

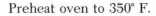

1 loaf french bread, unsliced

1/4 cup butter, melted

1 clove garlic, minced

2 dozen oysters

2 tablespoons butter for oysters

1/2 cup sour cream

1 tablespoon chopped parsley

Salt and pepper to taste

1/4 teaspoon celery seed

1/2 teaspoon paprika

For basting: melted butter containing 1 clove garlic, minced

Preheat oven to 350° F.

Cut off top third of french bread. Scoop out the center of bottom part and small amount of the top part.

Combine butter and garlic. Pour over the scooped-out bread pieces. Toast in oven, turning until well toasted.

Sauté the oysters in the butter until edges curl. Cut oysters in quarters. Add the sour cream, parsley, salt, pepper, celery seed, paprika, and toasted bread pieces. Mix by tossing.

Fill the bottom section of the scooped-out bread with the oyster mixture. Cover with the top section of the bread.

Bake 20 minutes or until golden brown. Brush top of bread with garlic butter every 5 minutes during baking time.

Put on hot serving dish and serve immediately.

THELMA'S FROG LEGS

SERVES 4

8 frog legs

Boiling water to cover

1 teaspoon salt

1/4 cup lemon juice

2 tablespoons melted butter

Salt and pepper to taste

1/4 cup shelled pumpkin seeds, ground

1/4 teaspoon horseradish

1 egg, beaten

Cracker crumbs for dredging

Cooking oil for deep frying

Only the hind legs of frogs are eaten. Skin the legs by scalding in the boiling, salted water with the lemon juice for about 2 minutes. Drain and dry the legs thoroughly.

Dip the legs in the melted butter. Roll in combination of salt, pepper, pumpkin seeds, and horseradish. Dip into beaten egg and then into the cracker crumbs.

Fry 3–4 minutes in deep cooking oil.

Serve 2 frog legs per person.

SOUTHERN OYSTERS

SERVES 4

4 cups (1 quart) oysters

Flour for dredging

2 tablespoons butter

1 1/2 tablespoons flour

Juice of 1 lemon

Salt and pepper to taste

1/4 teaspoon mace

1 teaspoon hot pepper sauce

Drain oysters for 1/2 hour. Save the liquid. Dredge oysters in flour.

Sauté oysters in the butter until edges curl. Remove oysters from pan.

Add the flour to the pan and stir well. Add oyster liquid, stirring constantly. Add lemon juice, salt, pepper, mace, and hot pepper sauce. Serve immediately.

Some oysters have more liquid than others. If more liquid is needed to make the sauce (last step) smooth and slightly runny, add milk.

AUSIEBELLE'S FRIED OYSTERS

SERVES 4

4 cups (1 quart) oysters

2 eggs, beaten

Salt and pepper to taste

1/4 teaspoon celery seed

Flour for dredging

Cracker crumbs for dredging

Butter for pan frying

Drain oysters. Save oyster liquid for another use.

Beat together the eggs, salt, pepper, and celery seed. Dredge oysters with flour. Dip in eggs. Dip in cracker crumbs.

Fry oysters quickly in butter. Drain on paper towels. Serve immediately.

FILLET OF FISH WITH SHRIMP STUFFING

SERVES 4

2 cups shrimp, cooked, shelled, deveined

2 eggs, beaten

1 cup sour cream

1/2 cup chopped mushrooms

Salt and pepper to taste

1/2 teaspoon paprika

1/4 teaspoon celery seed

1/4 teaspoon mustard

2 fish fillets (3 pounds)

1/4 cup sherry

Preheat oven to 350° F.

Mash shrimp into a paste. Mix eggs with half of the sour cream. Stir into shrimp paste. Add mushrooms, salt, pepper, paprika, celery seed, and mustard. Mix well.

Wash and dry the 2 fillets. Lay 1 fillet in oblong baking dish. Cover with shrimp mixture. Lay other fillet on top.

Sew the 2 fillets together with big stitches or tie with string. Pour over the fish the remaining sour cream mixed with the sherry. Bake 45 minutes. Remove the thread from the fish. Serve hot with lemon wedges.

LUCINDA'S FISH CAKES   SERVES 4

2 cups fish, boiled and well flaked

2 cups mashed potatoes

1 tablespoon butter

1 egg, beaten

Salt and pepper to taste

1 tablespoon poultry seasoning

Flour for dredging

Butter for frying

Any fresh fish that is suitable for boiling may be used, although codfish is preferred.

Mix fish together with mashed potatoes, butter, egg, and seasonings. Shape into round, flat cakes and dredge in the flour.

Fry on both sides in butter. Serve hot. Fish cakes are usually served with catsup.

BAKED SHAD

3–4 pounds shad, boned

1/2 cup melted butter

Salt and pepper to taste

1 teaspoon chopped parsley

Grated rind of 1 lemon

1 teaspoon mustard

2 tablespoons lemon juice

8–12 small potatoes, cooked

2 oranges, sliced

Preheat oven to 400° F.

Broil shad for 10 minutes in roasting pan, skin side up. Place in a buttered shallow pan skin side down. Pour melted butter over fish. Sprinkle with salt and pepper, parsley, lemon rind, and mustard.

Bake 15 minutes. Remove from oven and pour lemon juice over fish. Place potatoes around fish. Return to oven and bake 10–15 minutes, or until potatoes are browned and fish is well done. Don't overcook fish.

Garnish with orange slices. Serve hot.

Chapter 17
DESSERTS

Dessert was where Ausiebelle really loved to show off her creativity as a fine cook. It also gave her the opportunity to voice one of her dearly loved opinions. My mother and I knew it by heart, but that never stopped her famous pronouncements.

"Desserts should be like the end of a sermon. Heavy enough to stick with you, but light enough to remember the main scriptures."

It's at the end of a meal that people relax with strong coffee and some kind of sweet. Pies, tortes, custards, soufflés, and cakes were but a few of her specialties. Because Ausiebelle did her cooking in the South, a vast array of ingredients like huckleberries, peanuts, pecans, and various berries were always available to her.

I have enclosed some real family favorites to fill your kitchen with wonderful smells and to offer your family and friends the very best in Southern cuisine. As you close your meal with one of these delectable sweets, I hope you will remember the rich history that goes along with them.

Lucinda, Ausiebelle, and Thelma are but a few of the thousands of black women in history who have handed down their skills and expertise in the kitchen from generation to generation.

It is my dual hope that, by sharing these culinary delights, their tradition will be carried on, and the contributions of all these women will not be forgotten in our history.

HOT FROSTED GINGERBREAD

SERVES 6–8

1/2 cup butter

1/2 cup strong, hot coffee

2 eggs

1/2 cup sugar

1/2 cup molasses

3/4 (1/2) cup flour

2 teaspoons baking powder

1 teaspoon baking soda

1/2 teaspoon salt

1 teaspoon ginger

1 cup confectioner's sugar

4 tablespoons cream

1 teaspoon vanilla

Preheat oven to 350° F.

Melt the butter with the hot coffee. Beat the eggs and stir in the sugar and molasses. Combine this with the warm mixture. Sift and add the flour with the baking powder, soda, salt, and ginger.

Spread the batter in a greased and floured jelly-roll pan. Bake for 25 minutes. Remove from oven and, while still hot, frost with mixture of confectioner's sugar and cream, flavored with vanilla.

APPLESAUCE CAKE

SERVES 6–8

1/2 cup shortening

1/2 cup brown sugar

1/2 cup sugar

2 eggs

2 cups flour

1/2 teaspoon salt

1 teaspoon baking soda

1 teaspoon baking powder

1 teaspoon cinnamon

1/2 teaspoon nutmeg

1/4 teaspoon ground cloves

1 1/2 cups applesauce

1/2 cup chopped walnuts

1/2 cup chopped raisins

Preheat oven to 350° F.

In a large mixing bowl, cream together the shortening and sugars until light and fluffy. Add the eggs and beat well.

Sift together the flour, salt, soda, baking powder, cinnamon, nutmeg, and cloves. Add to the creamed mixture, alternating with the applesauce. Beat well after each addition.

Stir in the nuts and raisins. Spread the batter in a greased and floured 13 × 9-inch baking pan.

Bake for 35 minutes, or until a toothpick inserted in the center comes out clean.

APPLE DUMPLINGS   SERVES 4–6

1 cup flour

2 teaspoons baking powder

1/2 teaspoon salt

4 tablespoons shortening

1/4 cup water

1/4 teaspoon cinnamon

6–8 apples, peeled and sliced

Sauce

Preheat oven to 350° F.

Combine the flour, baking powder, and salt in a large bowl. Cut in the shortening until mixture resembles coarse crumbs. Sprinkle with the water and blend with a fork to form a dough.

On a floured surface, roll out the dough into a rectangle 1/8 inch thick. Sprinkle with cinnamon. Spread the apples over the dough. Roll it up, jelly-roll fashion, starting from the long end, to make a fat log.

Cut the roll into slices about 1 inch wide and place them on their sides in a buttered and floured baking pan.

Sauce:

> 2 cups water
>
> 1 tablespoon butter
>
> 1 1/2 cups sugar

Combine all the sauce ingredients and bring to a boil. Cool slightly.

Pour sauce over the dumplings. Fill the baking pan to within 1/2 inch of the top. Bake the dumplings 25–30 minutes.

RICE CUSTARD

SERVES 4–6

> 1/2 cup brown sugar
>
> 2 cups cooked rice
>
> 3 tablespoons melted butter
>
> 1 cup milk
>
> 3 eggs, beaten slightly
>
> 1/2 cup raisins
>
> 1/2 teaspoon vanilla
>
> Dash of nutmeg

Preheat oven to 350° F.

Add sugar to rice with butter, milk, and eggs. Place in deep baking dish. Set dish in a baking pan with enough water to come halfway up the sides of the dish.

Bake for 1 hour. When half done, remove from oven and add the raisins and vanilla. Sprinkle with nutmeg, then replace in oven and continue baking.

Serve hot or cold.

SOUTHERN CARROT PUDDING

SERVES 4–8

> 2 tablespoons butter
>
> 1 cup sugar
>
> 2 eggs, well beaten
>
> 1 1/2 cups grated raw carrots
>
> 1/4 teaspoon ground cloves

1/4 teaspoon nutmeg

1/2 teaspoon cinnamon

1 cup flour

Grated rind of 1 lemon

Grated rind of 1 orange

1/4 teaspoon salt

1 teaspoon baking soda

1 cup grated raw potatoes

1/4 pound citron, thinly sliced or diced

Cream butter and sugar. Add eggs, beating well. Add carrots, cloves, nutmeg, cinnamon, flour, lemon and orange rinds, and salt.

Sprinkle soda over potatoes and mix. Add to carrot mixture. Add the citron.

Butter the pudding mold and place a sheet of greased paper on the bottom. Pour in the pudding. Cover the mold and place on a rack in a pan of boiling water with a tight-fitting lid to steam for about 2 hours.

This pudding can be served with sweetened whipped cream or your favorite sauce.

MOLASSES PUDDING   SERVES 6–8

1 egg

2 tablespoons sugar

1/2 cup molasses

2 tablespoons melted butter

1/2 cup boiling water

1 1/2 cups flour

Pinch of salt

1 teaspoon baking soda

Foaming Sauce

Beat the egg and sugar until light and fluffy. Add the molasses, butter, and water. Beat in the sifted flour, salt, and baking soda.

Put in top of double boiler and let steam, covered for 1 hour. Serve with Foaming Sauce.

Foaming Sauce:

> 1 cup butter
>
> 2 cups powdered sugar
>
> 2 egg whites
>
> 1/3 cup rum
>
> 1/4 cup boiling water

Beat the butter, in a bowl, to a soft substance and gradually cream the sugar into it. Gradually add the unbeaten whites of eggs. Beat well. Add the rum. Beat well.

When light and smooth, gradually add the boiling water, beating all the time.

Place the bowl in a basin of hot water and stir about 2 minutes or until sauce is foamy.

Serve hot or cold on puddings.

HOT WATER PIECRUST

MAKES 2 CRUSTS

> 3/4 cup shortening
>
> 1/4 cup boiling water
>
> 1 tablespoon milk
>
> 2 cups bread flour
>
> 1 teaspoon salt

In a large bowl mix the shortening, boiling water, and milk. Whip with a fork until smooth and thick, the consistency of whipped cream.

Sift the flour and salt. Add to the liquid all at once, beating with the fork. Use the hands to mix and gather the dough together. Divide the dough into 2 balls.

Roll out 1 ball on a floured surface. Protect the other ball from drying out with a damp towel.

Makes enough dough for a 2-crust 9-inch pie. To make one pie shell, cut ingredients in half.

JACKSON CHERRY PIE

MAKES 1 PIE

1 cup sugar

3 tablespoons cornstarch

1/4 teaspoon salt

2 cans (1 pound each) pitted red cherries with juice

1/4 teaspoon red food coloring

Dash of almond extract

2 tablespoons butter

1 recipe Hot Water Piecrust

Preheat oven to 425° F.

In a saucepan mix the sugar, cornstarch, and salt. Stir in the cherry juice, coloring, and almond extract to make a smooth mixture. Simmer and stir over low heat until thick and clear.

Remove from heat and stir in the cherries and butter.

Roll out half of the piecrust and line a 9-inch pie pan. Pour the cherry mixture into the pastry shell. Roll out the remaining pastry and cut it into strips. Cover the cherries with strips of pastry, interlacing them in lattice fashion. Trim and crimp the edges.

Bake the pie for 40 minutes. Put a sheet of foil on the shelf under the pie to catch any drips.

Let the pie cool for about 30 minutes before serving.

DEEP SOUTH PUMPKIN PIE

MAKES 2 PIES

3 cups pumpkin, cooked or canned

3 cups evaporated milk

1 1/2 cups sugar

4 eggs, beaten

1/2 teaspoon salt

3/4 teaspoon ginger

1 teaspoon allspice

2 teaspoons cinnamon

1 recipe Hot Water Piecrust

Preheat oven to 450° F.

Combine and beat for 2 minutes the pumpkin, milk, sugar, eggs, salt, ginger, allspice, and cinnamon.

Roll out piecrusts on floured surface. Place in pie pans. Divide the pumpkin mixture between the 2 pie shells.

Bake for 15 minutes. Reduce heat to 375° and bake for another 45 minutes, or until a knife inserted near the center comes out clean.

Serve hot or cold.

LEMON CHESS PIE

MAKES 1 PIE

1/2 cup butter

2 cups sugar

5 eggs

1 cup milk

1 tablespoon flour

1 tablespoon white cornmeal

1/4 cup lemon juice

Grated rind of 3 lemons

1 recipe Hot Water Piecrust

Preheat oven to 350° F.

In a large mixing bowl, cream together the butter and sugar. Mix in the eggs. Beat well. Add the milk. Beat well. Add the flour, cornmeal, lemon juice and rind. Pour mixture into the pie shell.

Bake for 50 minutes.

LUCINDA'S PECAN PIE

MAKES 1 PIE

2 tablespoons butter

1 cup sugar

1 cup dark corn syrup

2 eggs, beaten

1 cup pecan meats, unbroken

1 teaspoon vanilla

1 recipe Hot Water Piecrust, see page 156

Whipped cream

Preheat oven to 275° F.

Cream the butter and sugar. Add the syrup, the beaten eggs, pecans, and vanilla. Beat well together.

Pour into unbaked pie shell. Bake for about 30 minutes. Test with a silver knife. Pie is done when knife comes out clean after being inserted into the center.

Serve with whipped cream.

AUSIEBELLE'S PANDOWDY   MAKES 1 PIE

6 apples

Cold water to cover

1½ cups molasses

1 teaspoon nutmeg

2 teaspoons cinnamon

½ teaspoon ground cloves

Pandowdy Piecrust

Preheat oven to 350° F.

Core and pare the apples and cut into small pieces. Cover with cold water and let stand for 10 minutes. Drain and place apples in buttered metal baking dish or ceramic that can be used over direct heat.

Cover apples with molasses, nutmeg, cinnamon, cloves. Cover the top with piecrust.

Bake for about 1 hour, or until crust is light brown.

When pie is cold, break the crust into the apple mixture. Place over low heat and simmer a few minutes.

Chill and serve with whipped cream.

Pandowdy Piecrust:

1½ cups bread flour

½ cup butter

1¼ cups milk

Put the flour into a mixing bowl. Cut in the butter until mixture resembles coarse crumbs. Sprinkle with the milk and blend with a fork to form a dough.

Lay dough on a floured surface and roll out in the shape of a pie plate. Lift gently and place in pie plate.

CURDS AND CREAM

Set sour or rich, raw milk in a covered crock or bowl until it becomes clabber (curdles).

Pour slowly into a curd press until press is full. Place press in pan and let it drain overnight. A colander lined with a double thickness of cheesecloth may be used in place of the curd press.

In the morning, turn out onto a flat dish. Grate nutmeg freely over the top.

Serve with heavy sweet cream, more grated nutmeg, and sugar.

GOOBER BRITTLE

2 cups sugar

1 teaspoon baking powder

1 1/2 cups peanuts, shelled

Melt the sugar in a heavy iron pan directly over a very low heat. Don't stir. The sugar will finally turn brown as it caramelizes. Add the baking powder just before removing from heat. Add the peanuts and mix quickly. Spread immediately on a plate to harden and cool.

When cool, break into bite-size pieces.

TRADITIONAL HARD SAUCE   MAKES 3/4 CUP

1/2 cup butter

1 cup powdered sugar

Pinch of salt

1 teaspoon vanilla or brandy

Cream together the butter, sugar, and salt. Work in the vanilla or brandy.

Refrigerate and serve cold with hot puddings.

BRANDY SAUCE FOR PUDDINGS

3/4 cup water

1/2 cup brandy

Sugar to taste

1/2 teaspoon grated nutmeg

Mix all the ingredients in a saucepan. Bring to a boil, stirring.
Serve very hot on puddings.

INDEX

Chicken and Fruit Salad, 66–67

Griddle Cakes, 37

Grits, 35
  fried, 35

Gumbos
  Chicken Gumbo, 27
  Chicken Oyster Gumbo, 30
  Shrimp Gumbo, 29
  See also Soups

H

Ham
  Baked Ham, 94
  Baked Ham and Apple, 95
  Broiled Ham, 94
  Dixie Veal, Ham, and Cheese Rolls, 103
  Ham and Pineapple, 95–96
  Lucinda's Ham Shoulder, 96
  Raisin Sauce for, 115
  See also Pork

Hamburger-Bacon Roast, 85

Hamburger steaks, broiled, 84

Hard Sauce, 160

Hash Brown Potatoes, 61

Hoecakes, 36–37

Hollandaise Sauce, 113

Hominy Grits, 35

Horseradish Sauce, 112–13

Hot beverages
  Linda's Special Cider, 6
  Southern Tom and Jerry, 7

Hot Frosted Gingerbread, 152

Hot Water Piecrust, 156

I

Iced Mint Tea, 6

J

Jackson Cherry Pie, 157

Juleps, 4

L

Lamb
  Barbecued Lamb Shank Dinner, 76–77
  Barbecued Leg of Lamb, 75
  Frozen Mint Ice for Lamb, 115

LaMont's Authentic Barbecue, xiii

LaMont's Oyster Loaf, 144

LaMont's Roast Duck, 127–28

Lane, Issac, xi

Lane College, Jackson, Tennessee, xi–ii

Leftover Beef Casserole, 88

Leg of Veal Roast, 106

Lemon Chess Pie, 158

Lemon Sauce, for Corn Fritters, 36

Lima beans
  Brunswick Stew, 26
  fresh, 58
  See also Beans

Linda's Dried Beef, 84

Linda's Hollandaise Sauce, 113

Linda's Special Cider, 6

Linda's Veal Fricassee, 102

Liver LaMont, 87

Livers, chicken, eggs stuffed with, 46
Loafin' Cocktail, 7
Louisiana Molded Crabmeat, 12
Louisiana Veal Chops, 104–5
Louisiana Waffles, 39
Lucinda's Barbecue Sauce, 112
Lucinda's Chicken Casserole, 121
Lucinda's Fish Cakes, 147
Lucinda's Ham Shoulder, 96
Lucinda's Pecan Pie, 158–59
Lucinda's Scrapple, 97–98

M

Macklin, Lucinda, xi–ii, 55–56
 barbecue sauce, 73
Main meal, 19
Maryland Cream of Crab Soup, 23
Maryland fried chicken, 120
Mayonnaise, 68–69
Meat
 Ausiebelle Salad, 66
 barbecued, 73–74
  Barbecued Beef Bones, 78
  Barbecued Beef Brisket, 77
  Barbecued Lamb Shank Dinner, 76–77
  Barbecued Leg of Lamb, 75
  Barbecued Pork Chops, 80
  Chuck Steak Barbecue, 76
  Easy Beef Barbecue, 78–79
  Oven-Barbecued Short Ribs, 79
 sauces for, 111
  Frozen Mint Ice for Lamb, 115

Horseradish Sauce, 112–13
Linda's Hollandaise Sauce, 113
Lucinda's Barbecue Sauce, 112
Mushroom Sauce, 114
Raisin Sauce for Ham, 115
Tomato Sauce, 114
White Sauce, 113
See also Beef; Chicken; Lamb; etc.
Mint
 Iced Mint Tea, 6
 Mint Ice for Lamb, 115
 Mint Julep, 4
Miss Ausiebelle's Chicken Pot Casserole, 120
Molasses Pudding, 155–56
Molded dishes
 Grapefruit Ring Salad, 68
 Louisiana Molded Crabmeat, 12
 Shrimp Mold, 142–43
Mulatto Rice, 50
Mushrooms
 Earthy Veal Cutlets, 106–7
 Leg of Veal Roast, 106
 Mushroom Sauce, 114
 Sweetbreads and Mushrooms, 87–88
 Veal Chops in Buttered Paper, 104
 Wild Rice and Mushrooms, 48

N

New Orleans Eggs, 45
New Year's, Chitterlings for, 93

O

Okra
  Brunswick Stew, 26
  Chicken Gumbo, 27
  Chicken Oyster Gumbo, 30
  Okra and Tomatoes, 62
  Okra Soup, 22
  Shrimp Gumbo, 29
Omelet, Creole, 46–47
Opossum, 126–27
Oranges
  Chicken and Fruit Salad, 66–
    67
  Orange Julep, 4
Oven-Barbecued Short Ribs, 79
Oysters
  Ausiebelle's Fried Oysters,
    146
  Chicken Oyster Gumbo, 30
  LaMont's Oyster Loaf, 144
  Oyster Stew, 27
  Oyster Stuffing, 136
  Pigs in a Blanket, 14
  Southern Oysters, 145

P

Pandowdy, 159
Papaya
  Baked Papaya, 57
  Papaya Cocktail, 13
Parsnips and Salt Pork, 61
Partridge, roast, 128
Pastry
  for Beef Picnic Tarts, 86
  Hot Water Piecrust, 156
  for Pigeon Pie, 129
Peanut brittle, 160
Pecan Pie, 158–59
Peppers

  green
    Beef Picnic Tarts, 86
    Curried Rice, 50
  sweet red
    Shrimp Gumbo, 29
Picnic tarts, 86
Pies
  Ausiebelle's Pandowdy, 159
  Deep South Pumpkin Pie,
    157–58
  Jackson Cherry Pie, 157
  Lemon Chess Pie, 158
  Lucinda's Pecan Pie, 158–59
  Pigeon Pie, 129
Pigeon Pie, 129
Pigs in a Blanket, 14
Pineapple
  Ham and Pineapple, 95–96
  Rice and Pineapple
    Casserole, 51
Planter's Punch, 5
Ponce de Leon eggs, 47
Pones, 58
Pork
  Barbecued Pork Chops, 80
  Breaded Pork, 97
  Chitterlings, 93
  Lucinda's Scrapple, 97–98
  Parsnips and Salt Pork, 61
  preserving of, 91
  Roast Suckling Pig, 92
  See also Ham
Potatoes
  Ausiebelle Salad, 66
  Baked Shad, 148
  Barbecued Lamb Shank
    Dinner, 76–77
  Beef Picnic Tarts, 86
  hash brown, 61
  Potato Stuffing, 136
Pot Likker, 20
Potlikkers, 19
  See also Soups

Puddings
  Brandy Sauce for, 161
  Corn Pudding, 59
  Molasses Pudding, 155–56
  Southern Carrot Pudding,
    154–55
Pumpkin Pie, 157–58

Q

Quick Eggnog, 8

R

Rabbit
  Ausiebelle's Belgian Hare,
    126
Raisin Sauce for Ham, 115
Rice, 48
  Curried Rice, 50–51
  Grandmother's Veal, 107–8
  Mulatto Rice, 50
  Rice and Chicken Casserole,
    49
  Rice and Pineapple
    Casserole, 51
  Rice Custard, 154
  Rice Waffles, 39
  Shrimp and Rice Croquettes,
    143
  Shrimp Gumbo, 29
  Thelma's Rice Croquettes, 49
  Wild Rice and Mushrooms,
    48
Rich Pastry, for Pigeon Pie, 129
Roasted meats
  Leg of Veal Roast, 106
  Roast Duck, 127–28

Roast Partridge, 128
Roast Squab with Rice, 130
Roast Suckling Pig, 92

S

Salads, 65
  Ausiebelle Salad, 66
  Chicken and Fruit Salad, 66–
    67
  Cinnamon Apple Salad, 67
  Grapefruit Ring Salad, 68
  Mayonnaise for, 68–69
  Thelma's Sour Cream
    Dressing, 69
Salt pork, parsnips and, 61
Sauces
  Apple Ball Sauce, 92–93
  for Apple Dumplings, 153
  barbecue, 73–74
  Brandy Sauce for Puddings,
    161
  Brown Sauce, for Linda's
    Veal Fricassee, 102
  foaming, for Molasses
    Pudding, 156
  lemon, for Corn Fritters, 36
  Mayonnaise, 68–69
  for meat, 111
    Frozen Mint Ice for Lamb,
      115
    Horseradish Sauce, 112–13
    Linda's Hollandaise Sauce,
      113
    Lucinda's Barbecue Sauce,
      112
    Mushroom Sauce, 114
    Raisin Sauce for Ham, 115
    Tomato Sauce, 114
    White Sauce, 113
  Traditional Hard Sauce, 160

Okra Soup, 22
Parsnips and Salt Pork, 61
Pot Likker, 20
Shrimp Gumbo, 29
Southern Corn Custard, 60
String Beans and Bacon, 59
Sweet Potato Pone, 58
Thelma's Creole Beef Stew, 25
Turnip greens, for Pot Likker, 20
See also Beans; Tomatoes; etc.
Vegetarians, 43
Virginia Waffles, 40

W

Waffles
  Louisiana Waffles, 39
  Rice Waffles, 39
  Virginia Waffles, 40
Welsh Rarebit, 14
White Sauce, 113
Wild Rice and Mushrooms, 48
World War II, xii

Y

Yams, candied, 60